The Early Modern Englishwoman:
A Facsimile Library of Essential Works

Series II

Printed Writings 1641–1700: Part 4

Volume 2

Sarah Fyge Egerton

Advisory Board:

Margaret J.M. Ezell
Texas A & M University

Elaine Hobby
Loughborough University

Suzanne W. Hull
The Huntington Library

Barbara K. Lewalski
Harvard University

Stephen Orgel
Stanford University

Ellen Rosand
Yale University

Mary Beth Rose
University of Illinois, Chicago

Hilda L. Smith
University of Cincinnati

Retha M. Warnicke
Arizona State University

Georgianna Ziegler
The Folger Shakespeare Library

Patrick Cullen: Editor Emeritus

The Early Modern Englishwoman:
A Facsimile Library of Essential Works

Series II

Printed Writings 1641–1700: Part 4

Volume 2

Sarah Fyge Egerton

Selected and Introduced by
Robert C. Evans
with MeKoi Scott

General Editors
Betty S. Travitsky and Anne Lake Prescott

LONDON AND NEW YORK

First published 2012 by Ashgate Publishing

2 Park Square, Milton Park, Abingdon, Oxfordshire OX14 4RN
711 Third Avenue, New York, NY 10017

Routledge is an imprint of the Taylor & Francis Group, an informa business

First issued in paperback 2018

The Introductory Note and text notes copyright Robert C. Evans © 2012

All rights reserved. No part of this book may be reprinted or reproduced or utilised in any form or by any electronic, mechanical, or other means, now known or hereafter invented, including photocopying and recording, or in any information storage or retrieval system, without permission in writing from the publishers.

Notice:
Product or corporate names may be trademarks or registered trademarks, and are used only for identification and explanation without intent to infringe.

British Library Cataloguing-in-Publication Data
Egerton, Sarah Fyge.
  Sarah Fyge Egerton. – (The early modern Englishwoman : a facsimile library of essential works. Series II Printed writings, 1641–1700, Part 4)
  I. Title II. Series III. Evans, Robert C.
  821.4–dc23

Library of Congress Control Number: 2012934805

The image reproduced on the title page and on the cover is from the frontispiece portrait in Poems. *By the Most Deservedly Admired Mrs. Katherine Philips* (1667). Reproduced by permission of the Folger Shakespeare Library, Washington DC.

ISBN 978-0-7546-3116-3 (hbk)
ISBN 978-1-138-37873-5 (pbk)

CONTENTS

Preface by the General Editors

Introductory Note

Female Advocate: OR, AN ANSWER TO A Late SATYR AGAINST The Pride, Lust and Inconstancy, &c. OF WOMAN. *Written by a Lady in Vindication of her Sex* (1686; ESTC R 16722)

THE Female Advocate: OR, AN ANSWER TO A LATE SATYR Against the Pride, Lust and Inconstancy OF WOMAN. *Written by a Lady in Vindication of her Sex* (1707; ESTC T191079)

POEMS ON Several Occasions, Together with a PASTORAL. By Mrs. *S.F.* (1703; ESTC T125148)

PREFACE
BY THE GENERAL EDITORS

Until very recently, scholars of the early modern period have assumed that there were no Judith Shakespeares in early modern England. Much of the energy of the current generation of scholars has been devoted to constructing a history of early modern England that takes into account what women actually wrote, what women actually read, and what women actually did. In so doing, contemporary scholars have revised the traditional representation of early modern women as constructed both in their own time and in ours. The study of early modern women has thus become one of the most important – indeed perhaps the most important – means for the rewriting of early modern history.

The Early Modern Englishwoman: A Facsimile Library of Essential Works is one of the developments of this energetic reappraisal of the period. As the names on our advisory board and our list of editors testify, it has been the beneficiary of scholarship in the field, and we hope it will also be an essential part of that scholarship's continuing momentum.

The Early Modern Englishwoman is designed to make available a comprehensive and focused collection of writings in English from 1500 to 1750, both by women and for and about them. The three series of *Printed Writings (1500–1640, 1641–1700, and 1701–1750)* provide a comprehensive if not entirely complete collection of the separately published writings by women. In reprinting these writings we intend to remedy one of the major obstacles to the advancement of feminist criticism of the early modern period, namely the limited availability of the very texts upon which the field is based. The volumes in the facsimile library reproduce carefully chosen copies of these texts, incorporating significant variants (usually in the appendices). Each text is preceded by a short introduction providing an overview of the life and work of a writer along with a survey of important scholarship. These works, we strongly believe, deserve a large readership – of historians, literary critics, feminist critics, and non-specialist readers.

The Early Modern Englishwoman also includes separate facsimile series of *Essential Works for the Study of Early Modern Women* and of *Manuscript Writings*. These facsimile series are complemented by *The Early Modern Englishwoman 1500–1750: Contemporary Editions*. Also under our general editorship, this series includes both old-spelling and modernized editions of works by and about women and gender in early modern England.

New York City
2012

INTRODUCTORY NOTE

Sarah Fyge Egerton (1668–1723) is an intriguing poet for various reasons. In the first place, she wrote a great deal of poetry during a period when women poets were relatively rare. Her career as a poet also began at an astonishingly early age: she was barely fourteen years old when she wrote a poem titled *Female Advocate* (as titled in the Huntington copy, or *THE Female Advocate*, as sometimes titled) that proved highly controversial when printed several years later. Egerton's poem was a response to the several times reprinted *Love given o're, or, A Satyr against the pride, lust, and inconstancy &c. of woman* (first printed in 1682; of disputed authorship, but probably by Robert Gould). When her reply was printed in London in 1686, it aroused the embarrassment and anger of Egerton's father. Nevertheless, a second edition of the poem soon appeared (in 1687), and throughout much of the rest of her life, even though her relations with men were often very complicated, Egerton used poetry to share her thoughts, vent her feelings, and participate, to a highly unusual degree, in the public discourse of her times. At the end of her life, we now find in her newly accessible will, Egerton herself felt that she had accomplished enough as a writer to be memorialized in Westminster Abbey alongside such other notable English poets as Chaucer, Spenser, and Cowley (Egerton, 'Will').

Most of what we know today about Egerton is due to the pioneering research of Jesyln S. Medoff, whose seminal articles of 1982 and 1989 and extremely valuable although unpublished dissertation of 1994 are major sources of information about Egerton's life and works. Medoff's dissertation corrects the work of some other scholars as well as some of her own earlier work – all the more reason to regret that this substantial piece of scholarship, one on which I have relied heavily in this Introduction, is not more widely available. Noting in 1994 that her subject began life as Sarah Fyge, became Sarah Field when she married, and then even later became Sarah Egerton when she remarried, Medoff elects to refer to the poet as 'Sarah Fyge.' Yet most scholars and reference works call her 'Sarah Fyge Egerton', so that will also be my practice here.

Medoff's dissertation offers firm evidence (not least a December 20 baptismal record) that Egerton was born late in 1668, not in 1669, as Medoff herself had earlier suggested and as many standard sources continue to report – when not giving the date as 1670. Medoff was also able to show in 1994 that Sarah's father, Thomas Fyge (c. 1632–1705), after finishing his apprenticeship with the Company of Apothecaries in 1655, was then licensed as a doctor in 1661, and that by the time of his daughter's birth he was, as she puts it, 'a prominent London citizen' (1994, p. 35). Medoff was also able to identify Sarah's mother as Rebecca Alcock, not Mary Beacham (as some reference works report), to determine that she married Thomas Fyge in October of 1658 and that she was buried on 13 June 1672, and to clarify the number and sexes of the children she bore (perhaps six altogether, although only two – Thomas and Sarah – survived her). Thomas was twelve when his mother died; Sarah was three. (It seems worth noting that in recounting the details of this poet's life, Medoff's dissertation is at serious variance with Richard Greene's entry on Egerton in the 2004 *Oxford Dictionary of National Biography*; Greene cites the 1982 article but not the more accurate dissertation.)

After Rebecca's death, Thomas wed Mary Beacham (also spelled Beauchamp, but pronounced the same), a 'spinster' of twenty-five, and continued to father children, says Medoff, 'at the rate of about one every two years for the next fifteen years' (pp. 35–36). In a particularly intriguing paragraph, she reports that:

> Nothing more is known about Sarah's biological mother and very little about the woman who raised her, except one detail that could be quite significant. For his second wife, Thomas Fyge chose the granddaughter of Ralph Cudworth, the famous philosopher and leader of the Cambridge Platonists. This would make Mary Beacham the niece of Damaris, Lady Masham, essayist, poet, and close friend of John Locke. There is the possibility that Mary herself was well-educated, reared in a family that supported the idea of eloquent daughters. If so, she may have been a more important educational influence on Sarah than the father. (p. 36)

The death of Sarah's brother Thomas in 1677 left her, at not yet nine, Thomas Fyge's only surviving child from his first marriage. Indeed, of the many children Fyge then had with his wife Mary only five daughters survived into adulthood.

It was in 1686, less than a year after the death in infancy of Thomas's last son, that his daughter's poem *Female Advocate, or, an Answer to A Late Satyr Against The Pride, Lust, Inconstancy, &c. of Woman*, written several years earlier, now made its way into print, making her infamous in her father's eyes. The work was licensed for printing on June 2, 1686 and had been written, or so the author would later claim, in less than two weeks when she was 'scarce fourteen'. Although Egerton did not openly identify herself as the author, she did provide her initials ('S.F.'), and, as Medoff says, the title of the book 'can be read as a deliberate double entendre, advertising both the work and the author' as advocates for females (1994, pp. 21–22). A revised edition appeared in 1687. Though there seems little doubt that Egerton's father was displeased by the book's publication, the traditional story that in response he banished his daughter from London may not be true; there is, says Medoff, 'no documentary evidence' for it (1994, pp. 26–27). She may even have left of her own accord. In any case, although her decision to respond in writing to a male satirist was unusual, especially for so young a female, her poem is firmly in the *querelle des femmes* tradition initiated by the youthful Christine de Pisan.

Sometime in the late 1680s or early 1690s, Egerton reluctantly left London for Buckinghamshire, presumably to live at the Fyge family seat in Winslow. Not long after this move, it seems, she reluctantly married a Buckinghamshire lawyer named Edward Field. When he died in 1698 (not in the mid-1690s, as is sometimes said), he left 'Sarah a comfortable widow with a sizable estate and no children' (Medoff 1994, pp. 17, 94–95). She then found herself romantically attracted to a man named Henry Pierce, 'Edward Field's clerk and "dearest friend," who was apparently unresponsive to Fyge's advances and at some point also married'.

'This would-be adulterous crush' (Medoff continues) 'began soon after her first husband's death and continued well into her second marriage' (1994, pp. 106–07). It was only after Field's death that she once again began publishing poetry. In 1700 her elegy on the death of John Dryden was included in a commemorative collection titled *Luctus Britannici: or the Tears of the British Muses'*. (Nandini Bhattacharya mistakenly suggests that Egerton 'published' this entire volume [p. 220]; perhaps this should have read 'published in' the volume.) Later in 1700 Egerton contributed three more elegies on Dryden to *The Nine Muses*, a collection of poems by women. Revised versions of all these elegies from 1700 appear in her later collection, *Poems on Selected Occasions*.

This latter work implies a good deal about Egerton's social network at the turn of the century. Prefaced by commendatory verses probably written by the playwright Mary Pix, *Poems* includes works addressed to the philosopher John Norris, to the poet laureate Nahum Tate, to Elizabeth Bracegirdle (famed as the 'virgin actress'), to the actor George Powell, to the poet and translator John Yalden, and to the poet and classicist Joshua Barnes. As Medoff says, we cannot assume that Egerton personally knew all these addressees, but we can indeed deduce that she knew Barnes, that she had acquaintances in the world of the theater, and that 'she was an engaged reader of philosophical and scientific works' (Medoff 1994, p. 122).

Medoff provides a helpfully precise date for the next major event in Egerton's life – her marriage to Thomas Egerton. The date of this marriage has been variously reported: for Bhattacharya sometime in the '1690s' and for Greene sometime 'between 1700 and 1703'. Medoff, however, has located a Chancery Court record that dates it precisely to June, 1701, commenting that Sarah Egerton 'relinquished the relative liberty of widowhood in order to marry a country-dwelling man nearly twice her age, her distant cousin, the Reverend Thomas Egerton of Adstock, Buckinghamshire'. Their marriage (to put it mildly) was not happy. Medoff calls it 'a story of domestic violence, accusations of physical cruelty and infidelity, greed, dishonesty, family fragmentation, and a suit for divorce' (1994, p. 125). Thomas Egerton believed that his wife was withholding money from her first marriage – money that was now rightfully his. He also believed that she had, in Medoff's words, 'given or promised to give at least some of the estate to Henry Pierce'. The accusations and counter-accusations, as well as the legal records, are complicated; each party seems to have felt fully justified. The couple's relations quickly 'degenerated into acrimonious disputation and name-calling', as well as physical threats on both sides (Medoff 1994, pp. 136–39).

Sometime in 1703, in the midst of all this bitterness, Egerton's *Poems on Selected Occasions* was issued, and, since the volume contained poems mentioning her husband, its publication may have inflamed the marital situation. Medoff provides a detailed and well-documented account of the marriage's lengthy breakdown and also explains how the writer Delarivier Manley came to know of the affair and how she eventually ridiculed the Egertons in print between 1707 and 1711, even publishing some of Sarah Egerton's private letters in the process. Other significant events during this period included the death of Sarah Egerton's step-mother in the early summer of 1704 and the death of her father in March 1705 (Medoff 1994, pp. 140–43, 153 and 156).

Before his death, the elder Fyge had attempted, through the terms of his will, to engineer some kind of reconciliation between his daughter and her new husband. For whatever reasons, including the illegality of almost all divorce, the Egertons did manage to stay married for another decade and a half, although Sarah does not seem to have been happy, either in the marriage or in other respects. Her *Poems* apparently were not commercially successful, and her feud with Delarivier Manley continued for years, with Manley doing her best – repeatedly – to make a fool of her one-time friend. Egerton herself seems for the most part to have fallen into relative silence during the final period of her life. Evidence suggests that her husband was dead by 1720 and that she followed him on February 13, 1722/23 (Medoff 1982, pp. 172–73). A life that had begun with youthful outspokenness ended in relative quiet, if not in genuine peace.

Female Advocate: OR, AN ANSWER TO A Late SATYR AGAINST The Pride, Lust and Inconstancy, &c. OF WOMAN. *Written by a Lady in Vindication of her Sex* **(1686)**

THE Female Advocate: OR, AN ANSWER TO A LATE SATYR Against the Pride, Lust and Inconstancy OF WOMAN. *Written by a Lady in Vindication of her Sex* **(1707)**

Egerton's *Female Advocate* is perhaps her most famous single work. It was her very first publication and was printed thrice in her own lifetime – in 1686, in a revised edition in 1687, and once more in 1707. A facsimile version of the 1687 printing was edited and issued in print by Felicity Nussbaum in 1976, and various electronic editions of the text are widely available. Peter Merchant and Steven Orman recently produced a very handsome and richly annotated printed edition of the 1686 work in a series devoted to literary juvenilia.

The preface to the revised edition of 1687, often seen as an effort to soften her somewhat caustic tone, claims that Egerton had never intended her book to be published in its original form. The first printing, she asserts, relied on an uncorrected manuscript, and she even suggests that the (presumably male) compositors had changed or inserted words where the manuscript was illegible. The result was a poem she considered both faulty as a work of art and occasionally too sharply satirical for public consumption. Her modifications tried to rectify such shortcomings, but the new preface should not be viewed (as it sometimes is) as a significant surrender, for it is not only longer than the first but is often just as feisty. Thus, Egerton emphasizes her commitment to artistic integrity, implying her clear intention to correct the aesthetic flaws found in (or introduced into) the original printing. She refuses to concede that critics had influenced her decision to revise, claiming that she had never intended to publish some passages included in the original version. She also indicates that her effort at moderation partly responded to the recent and similar decision by Gould (if indeed Gould was the author) – a decision perhaps prompted in part by her effective counterattack. All in all, *Female Advocate*, especially in its first printing, is an astonishingly mature performance by an adolescent girl.

There seems at present no way to establish how – or why – the 1686 edition of *Female Advocate* came to be published, but the subject is intriguing. Medoff offers necessarily speculative, and sometimes alternative, suggestions in her 1982 article and her dissertation. She notes, for example, that Egerton herself claimed that she had not intended that the poem be published in 1686, posits that Egerton would not have risked angering her father by publishing a work that challenged conventional thinking, and discusses in some detail the considerable corrections and toning down of the 1687 edition over the earlier text. Perhaps the earlier version of the poem (written when Egerton was barely fourteen) had been circulating in MS among friends, and one of them published it without her permission. Medoff even raises the possibility, at one point, that Egerton may have had help in preparing the second edition and that the latter version may have been prepared when she was seventeen (1994; pp. 162–63).

Since the revised edition of 1687 has already been issued in the printed facsimile edited by Nussbam, there seems some merit in reprinting here the Huntington Library's copy of the original 1686 edition. (This is especially the case since the electronic reproduction of that copy in the Early English Books Online [EEBO] database is incomplete.) Also included in this volume is the third edition of 1707, which (as MeKoi Scott has helped confirm) is essentially a reprint – with very minor changes, mainly of capitalization or spelling – of the corrected edition of 1687. Copies of the 1707 edition are very rare – another reason for making it available here.

POEMS ON Several Occasions, Together with a PASTORAL. By Mrs. *S.F.* (1703)

In the introduction to her facsimile edition of *Poems on Several Occasions*, Constance Clark notes that the collection 'contains an admixture of styles and moods. Side by side with aggressive feminist manifestoes are lyrical poems that reveal Egerton's vulnerability to romantic love' (p. 3). Any attempt to label Egerton a particular 'kind' of writer would be defeated by the sheer diversity of her interests, topics, and tones. A mere glance at the table of contents will give some sense of the wide variety of issues covered in the collection, but it may also be useful here to give a more detailed overview of the topics that Egerton treats in these poems. Thus, the subject of the first poem, '*On Friendship*' (pp. 1–2), is obvious, but the title of the second, '*The Extacy*' (pp. 2–11), does not clearly reveal that the poem surveys the heavens and all aspects of the earth and that it rejects earthly corruptions (especially of cities and courts) and ends by commending rural life. '*On the Honourable Robert Boyl's, Notion of Nature*' (pp. 11–14) praises that philosopher and scientist for emphasizing the power of God rather than that of Nature, and the following '*Satyr against the Muses*' (pp. 14–16) cleverly mocks poetry and implies that Egerton herself began writing verses when she was eight. '*To the Queen*' (pp. 17–19) then offers Queen Mary II effusive poetic praise.

The following poem, '*The Liberty*' (pp. 19–21), demonstrates Egerton's freedom from convention, especially from the conventional rules applied to women. A poem to a named but so far unidentified recipient – '*To the Lady Cambell, with a Female Advocate*' (pp. 21–23) – offers crucial biographical claims about the composition and reception of Egerton's earliest poem. '*On my leaving London, June the 29*' (pp. 23–24) describes Egerton's departure from the capital after the controversy provoked by her first poem's publication. In '*The Repulse to Alcander*' (pp. 25–27) the rural speaker seems to imply that she had been sexually solicited by a man even though obligated to someone else. '*To Mr. Norris, on his Idea of Happiness*' (pp. 27–31) is a fairly effective poem praising the virtues of a rural life as opposed to the distractions of cities and courts. The brief poem that follows it – '*To one who in Love, set a Figure*' (p. 33) – advises a lover to examine his mistress, not astrology, for information about their relationship. Love, philosophy, utopianism, independence of thought – quite a range of subjects!

'*To Philaster*' (pp. 34–35) implies that a man who is now false was once the speaker's true love. In '*At my leaving Cambridge August the 14th, Extempore*' (pp. 35–36), the tone is sorrowful, but this is followed by '*To Orabella, Marry'd to an old Man*' (pp. 36–37), a clever, witty satire on the husband in a May/December marriage. In '*To Alexis, on his absence*' (pp. 38–39) a speaker expresses her frank desires for a young man. '*SONG*' (pp. 39), spoken by someone smitten with a careless swain, condemns constancy; a brief poem on '*Love*' (p. 40) wittily suggests that love is a universal passion that can be expressed even in religious verse; and the speaker in another '*SONG*' (pp. 40–41) frankly confesses to an interest in Phylaster and laments that he has abandoned her. '*To One who said I must not Love*' (pp. 42–43) admits to an inability to refrain from love and to an obsession with one attractive young man in particular. '*On the death of dear Statyra*' (pp. 44–45) laments the death of a young woman. '*On being ------ tax'd with Symony*' (pp. 46–47) mockingly defends getting money by making ecclesiastical appointments ('simony', an ancient abuse, was officially against the rules).

'*An occasional Copy, in Answer to Mr. Joshua Barns, Extempore*' (pp. 47–48) expresses gratitude for praise by Barnes (also addressed in *Poems* and identified earlier in this Introduction) but implies that she has not written for a while and has been long retired. '*Song on Madam S—*' (pp. 48–49) claims that wit is more attractive to men than physical beauty. '*The Fate*' (pp. 49–51) laments romantic mismatches, and the following '*SONG*' (p. 51) proclaims that love is most pleasant when forbidden or unknown. '*On a Gentleman and his Wife visiting a Lady*' (p. 52) wittily mocks a husband who fell asleep during the visit. '*The Vision*' (p. 53) offers a fairly frank account of a dream about a person named Alexis and his beauty. In *The Power of Love* (p. 55) the speaker confesses an interest in many men before giving a witty conclusion. '*To Marcella*' (p. 56) praises a young and beautiful actress who nevertheless manages to remain virtuous, and '*The Invocation*' (p. 58) asks for help in coping with lost love. Next is a poem (p. 60) praising an author for succinctly refuting atheism, and '*On Atheism*' then suggests that atheists are drunken debauchees who will ultimately suffer.

'*On a Sermon Preach'd Sept. the 6th, 1697. on these Words, You have sold your selves for Nought*' (pp. 64–65) mocks a minister for preaching like a lawyer;

'*A SONG*' (pp. 65–66) praises a woman's beauty; and then '*On my leaving S—y*' (p. 66) praises what is probably Surrey (a county just southwest of London) for providing refuge while the speaker was unpopular but suggests that she is now leaving it to pursue popularity. '*The Gratitude*' (pp. 68–70) claims that her grief is more worthy and sincere than that shown by hired elegists, and then '*On My Wedding Day*' (pp. 70–72) suggests that although her first marriage was forced she eventually grew to love her now-dead husband. '*The Fatality*' (pp. 72–73) describes how, trying to avoid one misfortune, she runs into others, and the lengthy '*Ode on the Death of Mr. Dryden*' (pp. 74–80) offers fairly conventional lamentation. '*The Advice*' (pp. 80–84) recommends living in the moment and not dwelling on the past or future. '*To Thyrsis on his Pastoral to Mr. Creech*' (pp. 84–86, probably referring to the scholar Thomas Creech) praises another poet's pastoral verse; '*Delia to Phraartes on his Playing Cæsar Borgia*' (pp. 86–88) praises an actor especially gifted at playing powerful men; and a third poem in this eulogistic series – '*To Clarona drawing Alexis's Picture and presenting it to me*' (pp. 88–90) – praises a female painter for exquisitely capturing Alexis even though he never sat for his portrait.

Another '*SONG*' (p. 90) laments that the speaker cannot help her passion for Exalis even though he loves others. In 'Erato *the Amorous Muse on the Death of* John Dryden, *Esq.*' (pp. 91–94) the muse of love poetry laments the death of Dryden; and then 'Delia *to* Phraartes *on his mistake of three Ladies writing to him*' (p. 94) praises the good looks of a male actor admired and praised by three women. '*To Marina*' (pp. 97–98) is a biting satire on a woman who hypocritically claims to be virtuous, and in 'Euterpe' (pp. 98–103) the muse of lyric poetry laments the loss of Dryden (a fine lyric poet, after all, if even more famous for drama and satire). In 'Terpsichore' (pp. 104–06) the muse of dance repeats the same pattern.

'*The Platonick*' (pp. 106–08) is on platonic love (still in the sense of idealized upward-moving adoration, not in the more diminished modern sense of non-sexual affection). '*The Emulation*' (pp. 108–09) is an assertive, clever rejection of female subjugation that expresses confidence in female artistic talent; and '*To Mr. Yalden, on his Temple of Fame,* Extempore' (pp. 110) praises the work of Thomas Yalden, poet and minister. '*On the Death of* William *III, King of* England' (pp. 111–14) remains curiously unfinished, but in '*To* N. Tate, *Esq; on his Poem on the Queen's Picture, Drawn by* Closterman' (pp. 114–15), Egerton praises a poem by Nahum Tate on a painting of the queen and alludes in passing to Edmund Spenser. In '*To my much valu'd Friend* Moneses' (pp. 116–17), Egerton praises a young but virtuous and talented male poet. The volume concludes with an appended pastoral poem titled 'The fond Shepherdess' in which a rustic maiden adeptly laments her unrequited love for Exalis (pp. 1–15).

As its title suggests, then, *Poems on Several Occasions, Together with a Pastoral* is a diverse volume with no obvious pattern or design. Successive poems sometimes seem to treat related themes; sometimes poems on opposite themes seem deliberately juxtaposed; and the collection also offers recurring themes or subjects, as in the several poems on Dryden, the numerous poems on love, and some examples of autobiographical verse. Some poems seem predictable, but many display real talent and can express surprisingly assertive or unexpected views. In sum, this collection deserves far more analytical attention than it has yet received.

Constance Clark's facsimile edition of this volume does not identify which copy is there reproduced. Clearly, however, it is not the one presently owned by the William Andrews Clark Memorial Library – the copy which, for the sake of variety, is reproduced here. It seems worth adding, moreover, that the Newberry Library owns a particularly interesting undated copy, one that contains a printed list of 'ERRATA' facing the first page of the Table of Contents. This list is not printed either in the copy that Constance Clark used for her facsimile nor in that owned by the Clark Library. Unfortunately, the Newberry copy is so badly faded, foxed, and damaged by age that it cannot be reproduced. However, I think that it may be useful here to supply the Newberry copy's list of errata, since the same printer's errors, sans list, appear on the corresponding pages in the Clark copy:

p. 9. l. 7:	*Theys* r. *These*
p. 12. l. 9:	*Sublumary* r. *Sublunary*
p. 13. l. 16:	*descartes and more* r. *Des-Cartes, and More*
p. 15. l. 9:	*Schreiks* r. *Shrieks*
p. 15. l. 10:	*Vesevius* r. *Vesuvius*
p. 16. l. 17:	*Plague* r. *Plagues*
p. 17. l. 7:	*With* r. *In*
p. 32. l. 4:	*secure* r. *serene*
l. 5:	*poor* r. *more*
p. 47. l. 9:	*Submisely* r. *submissly*
p. 63. l. 20:	*error* r. *errors*
p. 78. l. 19:	*fram'd* r. *fam'd*
p. 88. l. 14:	*tho'* r. *but*
p. 92. l. 12:	*sight* r. *sigh'd*
p. 95. l. 4:	r. *are*
p. 106. l. 10:	*unweary* r. *unwary*
p. 111. l. 18:	*thee* r. *their*
p. 113. l. 4:	*Tryton* r. *Trytons*
p. 115. l. 13:	*my* r. *thy*

The Newberry copy also contains many inked-in changes. Many of these corrections or additions are taken directly from the preceding list of errata, but some (interestingly) are not. (Once again, the page numbers in the Newberry copy on which these inked-in changes occur correspond to the page numbers of the Clark Library copy.) For example, on page 1, line 13, the word 'Such' has been inserted into the line, so that it reads as follows: 'Or in what Soul, is Such true kindly heat'. Similarly, on page 3, line 17, the word 'Rustive' has been changed to 'Loitering'. On page 10, line 9, 'slaugher'd' has been corrected as 'slaughter'd' and in line 10 'wast' has been changed to 'vast'. A small 'm' has been inserted next to the title of the poem '*To the Queen*' on page 17, while on page 89, line 10, 'long us'd' has been changed to 'Gaffled' (or 'Gattled'?). On page 114, the final two full lines of the poem on the death of King William have been crossed out. An illegible correction has been made in the third line from the bottom of page 8 of the concluding 'Pastoral', and, most interestingly, on the final page of the pastoral (p. 15), someone has indicated that the following words should be inserted after line 4: 'Transporting thought, then' [three further words illegible; possibly 'shall I &c'].

What are we to make of all these additional corrections and changes? The same hand that made them apparently also corrected most, but not all, of the listed errata, yet none of the changes reported in the preceding paragraph occurs in the errata list. Whoever made these additional changes felt entitled to alter words, cross out lines, and even insert an additional line. Could the hand that made these changes be the hand of Egerton herself? At present there is no way to answer this question with any certainty.

Acknowledgements

I wish to thank MeKoi Scott for his careful comparison of the 1687 and 1707 versions of *The Female Advocate*. Thanks are also due to Peter Merchant for kindly sending me a copy of the edition of *The Female Advocate* he co-edited with Steven Orman. I am very grateful to Carol Sommer of the Clark Library for her assistance and to Scott Jacobs of UCLA for his. I also wish to thank Kasia Drozdziak and Richard High of the University of Leeds. Finally, I am enormously grateful to the general editors, Betty Travitsky and Anne Lake Prescott, and to Jane Fielding of Ashgate, not only for their careful reading of the 'Introduction' but especially for their enormous patience with the various problems, particularly those relating to my health, which arose as this volume was being prepared. I could not have had collaborators who were more thoughtful (in every sense of the word), not only on this volume but on preceding volumes in this series.

References

ESTC R16722
ESTC T191079
ESTC T125148

Bhattacharya, Nandini (1998), 'Sarah Fyge Field Egerton', in Paul Schlueter and June Schlueter (eds), *An Encyclopedia of British Women Writers*, rev. ed., New Brunswick, NJ: Rutgers University Press, 219–21
Clark, Constance (1987), 'Introduction', *Poems on Several Occasions* (1703), by Sarah Fyge Egerton, Delmar, NY: Scholars' Facsimiles & Reprints, 3–10
Egerton, Sarah Fyge. 'Will of Sarah Fyge Egerton, 1721–2'. http://www.winslow-history.org.uk/winslow_will_egerton.shtm
Evans, Robert C. (2004), 'Sarah Fyge (Egerton), *The female advocate: or, An answer to a late sartyr against the pride, lust and inconstancy, &c. of woman* (1686)' in Helen Ostovich, Elizabeth Sauer, and Melissa Smiths (eds), *Reading*

Early Modern Women: An Anthology of Texts in Manuscript and Print, 1550–1700, New York: Routledge, 406–07

Greene, Richard (2004–10), 'Egerton [née Fyge; *other married name* Field], Sarah (1670–1723), poet', *Oxford Dictionary of National Biography* (Oxford: Oxford University Press; http://www.oxforddnb.com)

Medoff, Jeslyn (1994), '"My Daring Pen": The Autobiographical Poetry of Sarah Fyge (Field, Egerton), (1668–1723)' PhD Diss, Rutgers University

—— (1982), 'New Light on Sarah Fyge (Field, Egerton)', *Tulsa Studies in Women's Literature* 1.2: 155–75

—— (1989), 'Sarah Fyge', in Germaine Greer, Susan Hastings, Jeslyn Medoff, and Melinda Sansone (eds), *Kissing the Rod: An Anthology of Seventeenth-Century Women's Verse*, New York: Noonday Press, 345–53

Merchant, Peter and Steven Orman (eds) (2010), *The Female Advocate*, by Sarah Fyge Egerton, Sydney, Australia: Juvenalia Press

Nussbaum, Felicity (1976), (ed.), *Satires on Women*, Augustan Reprint Society: 180, Los Angeles: William Andrews Clark Memorial Library

ROBERT C. EVANS

Female Advocate: OR, AN ANSWER TO A Late SATYR AGAINST The Pride, Lust and Inconstancy, &c. OF WOMAN. *Written by a Lady in Vindication of her Sex.* (1686; ESTC R16722) is reproduced, by permission of The Henry E. Huntington Library (shelfmark 58338). The text block of the title page measures 184 × 130 mm. Text block of 'To the Reader' measures 183 × 130 mm.

Words or passages which are difficult to read:

10.23:	Are guilty
11.25:	And if by supposition I may go
11.26:	Then I'll suppose all men are wicked too,
12:24:	But I believe that you will let your hate
12:25:	Ore rule your bride, and you'll not vvish the State
13.4:	More then I speak of, think heaven design'd
13.5:	Them for a part of your Eternal Fate,
13.6:	Because they're things which you so much do hate.
14.1:	And that she's all that's pious, chast and true,
14.2:	Heroick, constant, nay, and modest too:
14.3:	The later Virtue is a thing you doubt,
14.4:	But 'tis 'cause you nere sought to find it out.
14.5:	You question where there's such a thing or no,
14.6:	'Tis only 'cause you hope you've lost a foe,
15.1:	And transmigrate them into others, and
15.2:	Still shift them as she finds the matters stand.
15.3:	'Tis 'cause they are the worst makes me believe
15.4:	You must imagine Jezabel and Eve.
15.5:	But I'm no Pythagorean to conclude
15.23:	But she's in such a state as she may fall,
15.24:	And without care her freedom may enthrall.
15.25:	But to keep pure and free in such a case,
15.26:	Argues each virtue with its proper grace.
15.27:	And as a womans composition is
15.28:	Most soft and gentle, she has happiness
15.29:	In that her soul is of that nature too,
15.30:	And yeilds [sic] to any thing that heaven will do,
21.1:	But I believe one might as narrowly pry
21.2:	For't, as the Grecian did for honesty,
22.5:	We have in Egypt's false King Ptolomy,
22.6:	Who, tho' he under obligations were,
23.7:	All Pride and Lust too to our charge they lay,

Female Advocate:
OR, AN
ANSWER
TO
𝔄 𝔏𝔞𝔱𝔢 𝔖𝔄𝔗𝔜𝔕
AGAINST
The Pride, Luft and Inconftancy, &c.
OF
WOMAN.

Written by a Lady in Vindication of her Sex.

Licens'd, June 2. 1686. R. P.

LONDON:
Printed by *H. C.* for *John Taylor*, at the *Globe* in St. *Paul's*-Church-Yard. 1686.

TO THE READER.

That which makes many Books come abroad into the World without Prefaces, is, the only Reason that incites me to one, viz. the Smalness of them; being willing to let my Reader know why this is so: For as one great Commendation of our Sex, is, to know much, and speak little, so my Virgin-Modesty hath put a Period to the intended Length of the ensuing Lines, lest censuring Criticks should measure my Tongue by my Pen, and condemn me for a Talkative, by the length of my Poem. Tho' I confess the Illustrious Subject requires (nay commands) an enlargement from any other Pen than mine (or those under the same Circumstances) but I think it is good Frugality for young Beginners to send forth a small Venture at first, and see how that passes the merciless Ocean of Criticks, and what Returns it makes, and so accordingly adventure the next time. I might enlarge this Preface with the common Excuse of Writers for the Publication of their Books, viz. the Importunities of her obliging Friends: But what it was put me upon the Publication of this, I am not bound to give the Reader an Account of; but I think the Debauchery which I now answer, is a sufficient warrant for this appearing of mine; in which he doth not only exclaim against Virtue, but Moral Honesty too, and would (were it alone sufficient) banish all Goodness out of them; but that will be an impossible thing, so long as we (the most essentially good) do subsist: for 'tis observed in all Religions, that Women are the truest Devotionists, and the most pious, and more heavenly than those who pretend to be the most perfect and rational Creatures; for many Men with the Conceit of their own Perfections, neglect that which should make them so; as some mistaken persons, who think if they are of the right Church they shall be infallibly saved, when they never follow the Rules which lead to Salvation; and when Persons with this Inscription pass currant in Heaven, then it will be according to my Antagonist's Fancy, that all Men are good, and fitting for Heaven because they are Men; and Women irreversibly damn'd, because they are Women: But that Heaven should make a Male and Female, both of the same Species, and both indued with the like Rational Souls, for two such differing Ends, is the most notorious Principle, and the most unlikely of any that ever was maintained by any Rational Man, and I shall never take it for an Article of my Faith, being assured that Heaven is for all those whose Purity and Obedience to its Law, qualifies them for it, whether Male or Female; to which Place the latter seem to have the Claim, is the Opinion of one of its Votaries,

S. F.

THE
Female Advocate,
OR,

An Answer to a late Satyr against the Pride, Lust and Inconstancy, &c. of Woman.

Blasphemous Wretch, who canst think or say
Some Curst or Banisht Fiend usurp't the way
When *Eve* was form'd; for then's deny'd by you
Gods Omniscience and Omnipresence too:
Without which Attributes he could not be,
The greatest and supreamest Deity:
Nor can Heaven sleep, tho' it may mourn to see
Degenerate Man utter Blasphemy.
When from dark *Chaos* Heav'n the World did make,
Made all things glorious it did undertake;
Then it in *Eden*'s Garden freely plac'd
All things pleasant to the Sight or Taste,
Fill'd it with Beasts & Birds, Trees hung with Fruit,
That might with Man's Celestial Nature suit:
The World being made thus spacious and compleat,
Then Man was form'd, who seemed nobly great.

When

When Heaven survey'd the Works that it had done,
Saw Male and Female, but found Man alone,
A barren Sex, and insignificant;
So Heaven made Woman to supply the want,
And to make perfect what before was scant:
Then surely she a Noble Creature is,
Whom Heaven thus made to consummate all Bliss.
Though Man had Being first, yet methinks She
In Nature should have the Supremacy;
For Man was form'd out of dull senceless Earth;
But Woman she had a far nobler Birth:
For when the Dust was purify'd by Heaven,
Made into Man, and Life unto it given,
Then the Almighty and All-wise God said,
That Woman of that Species should be made:
Which was no sooner said, but it was done,
'Cause 'twas not fit for Man to be alone.
Thus have I prov'd Womans Creation good,
And not inferior, when right understood:
To that of Man's; for both one Maker had,
Which made all good; then how could *Eve* be bad?
But then you'l say, though she at first was pure,
Yet in that State she did not long endure.
'Tis true; but if her Fall's examin'd right,
We find most Men have banish'd Truth for spight:
Nor is she quite so guilty as some make;
For *Adam* did most of the Guilt partake:
For he from God's own Mouth had the Command;
But Woman she had it at second hand:

The Devil's Strength weak Woman might deceive,
But *Adam* tempted only was by *Eve*.
Eve had the strongest Tempter, and least Charge;
Man's knowing most, doth his Sin make most large.
But though Woman Man to Sin did lead?
Yet since her Seed hath bruis'd the Serpent's Head:
Why should she be made a publick scorn,
Of whom the great Almighty God was born?
Surely to speak one slighting Word, must be
A kind of murmuring Impiety:
But still their greatest haters do prove such
Who formerly have loved them too much:
And from the Proverb they are not exempt;
Too much Familiarity has bred Contempt;
For they associate themselves with none,
But such whose Virtues like their own, are gone;
And with all those, and only those who be
Most boldly vers'd in their Debauchery:
And as in *Adam* all Mankind did die,
They make all base for ones Immodesty;
Nay, make the Name a kind of Magick Spell,
As if 'twould censure married Men to Hell.

Woman, ye Powers! the very Name's a Charm,
And will my Verse against all Criticks arm.
The *Muses* or *Apollo* doth inspire
Heroick Poets; but your's is a Fire,
Pluto from Hell did send by *Incubus*,
Because we make their Hell less populous;
Or else you ne'er had damn'd the Females thus:

But

But if so universally they are
Dispos'd to Mischief, what need you declare
Peculiar Faults, when all the World might see
With each approaching Morn a Prodigy:
Man curse dead woman; I could hear as well
The black infernal Devils curse their Hell:
When there had been no such place we know,
If they themselves had not first made it so.
In Lust perhaps you others have excell'd,
And made all Whores that possibly would yield;
And courted all the Females in your way,
Then did design at last to make a Prey
Of some pure Virgins; or what's almost worse,
Make some chaste Wives to merit a Divorce.
But 'cause they hated your insatiate Mind,
Therefore you call what's Virtuous, Unkind:
And Disappointments did your Soul perplex;
So in meer spight you curse the Female Sex.
I would not judge you thus, only I find
You would adulterate all Womankind,
Not only with your Pen; you higher soar;
You'd exclude Marriage, make the World a Whore.

But if all Men should of your Humor be
And should rob *Hymen* of his Deity,
They soon would find the Inconveniency.
Then hostile Spirits would be forc'd to Peace,
Because the World so slowly would increase.
They would be glad to keep their Men at home,
And each want more to attend his Throne;

Nay,

Nay, should an *English* Prince resolve that he
would keep the number of of's Nobility:
And this dull custom some few years maintain'd,
There would be none less than a Peer oth' land.
And I do fancy 'twould be pretty sport
To see a Kingdom cramb'd into a Court.
Sure a strange world, when one should nothing see,
unless a Baudy House or Nunnery.
Or should this Act ere pass, woman would fly
With unthought swiftness, to each Monastry
And in dark Caves secure her Chastity.
She only in a Marriage-Bed delights;
The very Name of *Whore* her Soul affrights.
And when that sacred Ceremony's gone,
VVoman I am sure will chuse to live alone.

There's none can number all those vertuous Dames
VVhich chose cold death before their lovers flames.
The chast *Lucretia* whom proud *Tarquin* lov'd,
Her he slew, her chastity she prov'd.
But I've gone further than I need have done,
Since we have got examples nearer home.
VVitness those *Saxon* Ladies who did fear
The loss of Honour when the *Danes* were here:
And cut their Lips and Noses that they might
Not pleasing seem, or give the *Danes* delight.
Thus having done what they could justly do,
At last they fell their sacrifices too.
Thus when curst *Osbright* courted *Beon*'s wife,
She him refus'd with hazard of her life.

B

And

And some which I do know but will not name,
Have thus refus'd and hazarded the same.
I could say more, but History will tell
Many more things that do these excel.

In Constancy they men excell as far
A heavens bright lamp doth a dull twinckling star.
Tho' man is alwaies altering of his mind,
Inconstancy is only in womankind.
'Tis something strange, no hold, it isn't because
The men have had the power of making Laws;
For where is there that man that ever dy'd,
Or ere expired with his loving Bride.
But numerous trains of chast wives expire
With their dear Husbands, tho in flames of fire:
We'd do the same if custom did require.
But this is done by *Indian* women, who
Do make their Constancy immortal too,
As is their Fame: We find *India* yeilds
More glorious *Phœnix* than the *Arabian* fields.
The *German* women Constancy did shew
When *Wensberg* was besieg'd, beg'd they might go
Out of the City, with no bigger Packs
Than each of them could carry on their Backs.
The wond'ring world expected they'd have gone
Laded with treasures from their native home,
But crossing expectation each did take
Her Husband as her burden on her back.
So saved him from intended death, and she
At once gave him both life and liberty.

           How

How many loving wives have often dy'd:
Drownded in tears by their cold husbands side.
And when a Sword was Executioner,
the very same hath executed her,
With her own hands; eagerly meeting death,
And scorn'd to live when he was void of breath.
If this isn't Constancy, why then the Sun
With Constant Motion don't his progress run.
There's thousands of examples that will prove,
Woman is alwayes Constant in chast Love.
But when she's courted only to some Lust,
She well may change, I think the reason's just.
Change did I say, that word I must forbear,
No, she bright Star wont wander from her sphere
Of Virtue (in which Female Souls do move)
Nor will she joyn with an insatiate love.
For she whose first espoused to vertue must
Be most inconstant, when she yields to lust.
But now the scene is alter'd, and those who
were esteemed modest by a blush or two,
Are represented quite another way,
Worse than mock-verse doth the most solid Play.
She that takes pious Precepts for her Rule,
Is thought by some a kind of ill-bred fool;
They would have all bred up in *Venus* School.
And when that by her speech or carriage, she
Doth seem to have sence of a Deity,
She straight is taxt with ungentility.
Unless it be the little blinded Boy,
That Childish god, *Cupid*, that trifling toy,

That

That certain nothing, whom they feign to be
The Son of *Venus* daughter to the Sea.
But were he true, none serve him as they shoud,
For commonly those who adore this god,
Do't only in a melancholy mood;
Or else a sort of hypocrites they are,
Who do invocate him only as a snare.
And by him they do sacred love pretend,
When as heaven knows, they have a baser end.
Nor is he god of love; but if I must
Give him a title, then he is god of lust.
And surely Woman impious must be
When e're she doth become his votary,
Unless she will believe without controul,
Those that did hold a Woman had no Soul:
And then doth think no obligation lyes
On her to act what may be just or wise.
And only strive to please her Appetite,
And to embrace that which doth most delight.
And when she doth this paradox believe,
Whatever faith doth please she may receive.
She may be Turk, Jew, Atheist, Infidel,
Or any thing, cause she need ne'er fear Hell,
For if she hath no Soul what need she fear
Something she knows not what or when or where.

But hold I think I should be silent now,
Because a Womans Soul you do allow.
But had we none you'd say we had, else you
Could never damn us at the rate you do.

What

What doſt thou think thou haſt priviledge given,
That thoſe whom thou doſt bleſs ſhall mount to (heaven
And thoſe thou curſeſt unto hell muſt go.
And ſo doſt think to fill the *Abiſs* below
Quite full of Females, hoping there may be
No room for ſouls big with Vice as thee.
But if that thou with ſuch vain hopes ſhould'ſt dye
I'th fluid Air, thou muſt not think to fly,
Or enter into heaven, thy weight of Sin
Would cruſh the damn'd, and ſo thoud'ſt enter in.
But hold, I am uncharitable here,
Thou may'ſt repent, tho' that's a thing I fear.
But if thou ſhould'ſt repent, why then again
It would at beſt but mitigate thy pain,
Becauſe thou haſt been vile to that degree,
That thy repentance muſt eternal be.
For wert thou guilty of no other crime
Than what thou lately putteſt into Rhime,
Why that without other offences given,
Were enough to ſhut the gate of Heaven.
But when together's put all thou do,
It will not only ſhut but bar it too.

For when Heaven made woman it deſign'd
Her for the charming object of Mankind.
Nor is alter'd only with thoſe who
Set *Bewly, Stratford,* nay and *Chreſwell* too,
Or other Bawds, chaſe their acquaintance out,
And then what they muſt be we make no doubt.
'Tis to make heaven miſtaken when you ſay

It

It meant one and it proves another way.
For when heaven with its laſt and greateſt care,
Had form'd a female charming bright and fair,
Why then immediately it did decree,
That unto man ſhe ſhould a bleſſing be,
And ſo ſhould prove to all poſterity.
And ſurely there is nothing can be worſe
Than for to turn a bleſſing to a curſe.
And when the greateſt bleſſing heaven ere gave,
And certainly the beſt that man could have.
When that's ſcorn'd and contemn'd ſure it muſt be
A great affront unto heaven's Majeſty.
But I hope Heaven will puniſh the offence,
And with it juſtifie our Innocence.

I muſt confeſs there are ſome bad, and they
Lead by an *Ignis fatus*, go aſtray :
All are not forc'd to wander in falſe way.
Only ſome few whoſe dark benighted ſence,
For want of light han't power to make defence
Againſt thoſe many tempting pleaſures, which
Not only theirs but Maſculine Souls bewitch.
But you'd perſuade us, that 'tis we alone
Are gulty of all crimes and you have none,
Unleſs ſome few, which you call fools, (who be
Eſpous'd to wives, and live in chaſtity.)
But the moſt rational without which we
Doubtleſs ſhou'd queſtion your Humanity.
And I would praiſe them more only I fear
If I ſhould do't it would make me appear

Unto

Unto the World much fonder than I be
Of that same State, for I love Liberty,
Nor do I think there's a necessity
For all to enter Beds, like *Noah*'s beast
Into his Ark ; I would have some releast
From the dear cares of that lawful State :
Hold I'll not dictate, I'll leave all Fate.
Nor would I have the World to think that I
Through a despair do *Nuptial Joys* defy.
For in the World so little I have been
That I've but half a revolution seen
Of *Saturn,* only I do think it best
For those who love to contemplate at rest,
For to live single too, and then they may
Uninterupted, *Natures Work* survey.
And had my Antagonist spent his time
Making true Verse instead of spiteful Rhime,
As a Female Poet, he had gain'd some praise,
But now his malice blasts his twig of Bays.
I do not wish you had, for I believe
It is impossible for to deceive
Any with what you write, because that you
May insert things supposed true.
And if by supposition I may go,
Then I'll suppose all Men are wicked too,
Because I'm sure there's many that are so.
And 'cause you have made *Whores* of all you could,
So if you durst, you'd say all Women would.
Which words do only argue guilt and spite :
All makes you cheap in ev'ry mortals sight.

          And

And it doth shew that you have alwaies been
Only with Women guilty of that Sin.
You nere desired nor were you fit for those
Whose modest carriage doth their minds disclose.
And Sir, methinks you do describe so well
The way and manner *Bewley* enter'd Hell,
As if your love for her had made you go
Down to the black infernal shades below.
But I suppose you never was so near,
For if you had, you scarce would have been here,
For had they seen, they'd kept you there.
Unless they thought when ere it was you came,
Your hot entrance might encrease the flame.
If burning Hell add to their extreme pain,
And so were glad to turn you off again.
And likewise, also I believe beside,
That one thing more might be their haughty pride.
They knew you Rival'd them in all their Crimes,
Wherewith they could debauch the willing times.
And as fond mortals hate a rival, they
Loving through Pride, were loath to let you stay,
For fear that you might their black deeds excel,
Usurp their Seat and be the Prince of Hell.
But I believe that you will let your hate
Ore rule your bride, and you'll not wish the State
Of Governing, because your deceived mind,
Persuades your Subjects will be Women kind.
But I believe when it comes the tryal,
Ask but for ten and you'll have the denial.

                                             You'd

You'd think your self far happier than you be,
Were you but half so sure of heaven as we.
But when you are in hell if you should find
More then I speak of, think heaven design'd,
Them for a part of your Eternal Fate,
Because they're things which you do much do hate,
But why you should do so I cannot tell,
Unless 'tis what makes you in love with hell:
And having fallen-out with Goodness, you
Must have Antipathy 'gainst Woman too.
For virtue and they are so near ally'd
That none can their mutual tyes divide.
Like Light and Heat, incorporate they are,
And interwove with providential care.
But I'm too dull to give my Sex due praise,
The task befits a Laureat Crown'd with Bays:
And yet all he can say, will be but small,
A Copy differs from the original.
For should he sleep under *Parnassus* Hill,
Implore the Muses for to guide his Quill.
And shou'd they help him, yet his praise would seem
At best but undervalluing disesteem.
For he would come so short of what they are
His lines won't with one single Act compare.
But to say truest, is to say that she
Is Good and Virtuous unto that degree
As you pretend she's Bad, and that's beyond
Imagination, 'cause you set no bound,
And then one certain definition is
To say that she doth comprehend all Bliss.

C   And

And that she's all that's pious, chaft and true,
Heroick, conftant, nay, and modeft too:
The later Virtue is a thing you doubt;
But 'tis 'caufe you nere fought to find it out.
You queftion where there's fuch a thing or no,
'Tis only 'caufe you hope you've loft a foe,
A hated object, yet a ftranger too.
I'll fpeak like you, if fuch a thing there be,
I'm certain that fhe doth not dwell with thee.
Thou art Antipodes to that and unto all
That's Good, or that we fimply civil call.
From yokes of Goodnefs, thou'ft thy felf releaft,
Turn'd Bully Hector, and a humane Beaft.
That Beafts do fpeak it rarely comes to pafs,
Yet you may paralell with *Balaam*'s Afs.
You do defcribe a woman fo that one
Would almoft think fhe had the Fiends outdone:
As if at her ftrange birth did fhine no ftar,
Or Planet, but Furies in conjunction were;
And did confpire what mifchief they fhould do,
Each act his part and her with plagues purfue,
'Tis falfe in her, yet 'tis fum'd up in you.
You almoft would perfwade one that you thought
That providence to a low ebb was brought;
And that to *Eve* and *Jezabell* was given
Souls of fo great extent that heaven was driven
Into a Straight, and liberality
Had made her void of wanting, to fupply
Thefe later bodies, fhe was forc'd to take
Their fouls afunder, and fo numbers make,

And

And transmigrate them into others, and
Still shift them as she finds the matters stand.
'Tis 'cause they are the worst makes me believe
You must imagine *Jezabel* and *Eve*.
But I'm no *Pythagoran* to conclude
One Soul could serve for *Abraham* and *Jude*.
Or think that heaven so bankrupt or so poor,
But that each body has one soul or more.
I do not find our Sex so near ally'd,
Either in disobedience or in pride,
Unto the 'bovenamed Females (for I'm sure
They are refin'd, or else were alwaies pure)
That I must needs conceit their souls the same,
Tho' I confess there's some that merit blame:
But yet their faults only thus much infer,
That we're not made so perfect but may err;
Which adds much lustre to a virtuous mind,
And 'tis her prudence makes her soul confin'd
Within the bounds of Goodness, for if she
Was all perfection, unto that degree
That 'twas impossible to do amiss,
Why heaven not she must have the praise of this.
But she's in such a state as she may fall,
And without care her freedom may enthrall.
But to keep pure and free in such a case,
Argues each virtue with its proper grace.
And as a womans composition is
Most soft and gentle, she has happiness
In that her soul is of that nature too,
And yeilds to any thing that heaven will do.

C 2   Takes

Takes an impression when 'tis seal'd in heaven,
Turns to a cold refusal, when 'tis given
By any other hand: She's all divine,
And by a splendid lustre doth outshine
All masculine souls, who only seem to be
Made up of pride and their lov'd luxury.
So great's mans ambition that he would
Have all the wealth and power if he could,
That is bestowed on the several Thrones
Of the worlds Monarchs, covets all their Crowns.
And by experience it hath been found
The word Ambition's not an empty sound.
There's not an History which doth not shew
Man's pride, ambition and his falshood too.
For if at any time th'ambitious have
Least shew of honour, then their souls grow brave,
Grow big and restless, they are not at ease,
'Till they have a more fatal way to please,
Look fair and true, when falsely they intend;
So from low Subject, grow a Monarch's Friend.
And by grave Councels they their good pretend,
When 'tis guilt poyson and oft works their end.
The Son who must succeed, is too much loved,
Must be pull'd down (his Councel is approved)
For fear he willingly should grow too great,
Desire to rule, should mount his father's Seat.
So he's dispatch'd, and then all those that be
Next in the way are his adherency.
And then the better to secure the State,
It is but just they should receive his fate.

So by degrees he for himself makes room,
His Prince is straightway shut up in his Tomb,
And then the false usurper mounts the Throne.
Or would do so at least but commonly
He nere sits firm, but with revenge doth dy, (high,
But thank heaven there's but few that reach so
For the known crimes makes a wise Prince take care.
Thus what I've said doth plainly shew there are
Men more impious than a woman far.
So those who by their abject fortune are
Remote from Courts no less their pride declare,
In being uneasie and envying all who be
Above them, in State, or Priority.
But 'tis impossible for to relate
Their boundless Pride, or their prodigious hate,
To all that fortune hath but smil'd upon,
In a degree that is above their own.
And thou proud fool, that virtue would'st subdue,
Envying all good, doft towre ore woman too,
Which doth betray a base ignoble mind,
Speaks thee nothing but a blustring wind.
But in so great a lab'rinth as man's pride,
I should not enter, nor won't be imply'd,
For to search out their strange and unknown crimes,
There's so many apparent in these times,
That my dull Arithmetick cannot tell
Half the sins that commonly do dwell
In one sordid Rustick, then how can I
Define the Courts or Towns Debauchery.

Their

Their pride in some small measure I have shown,
But theirs is running over and prest down;
And 'tis impossible I should repeat
The Crimes of men extravagantly great,
I would not name them, but to let them see
I know they'r bad and odious unto me
'Tis true, pride makes men great in their own eyes,
But them proportionable I despise;
And tho' Ambition still aims to be high,
Yet Lust at best is but beastiality;
A Sin with which there's none can compare,
Not Pride nor Envy, &c. for this doth insnare,
Not only those whom it at first inflam'd,
This Sin must have a partner to be sham'd,
And punish'd like himself.   Hold, one wont do,
He must have more, for he doth still pursue
The Agents of his Passion; 'tis not Wife,
That Mutual Name can regulate his Life:
And tho' he for his Lust might have a shrowd,
And there might be *Poligamy* allow'd,
Yet all his Wives would surely be abhorr'd,
And some common *Lais* be ador'd.
Most mortally the Name of Wife they hate,
Yet they will take one as their proper fate,
That they may have a Child legitimate,
To be their Heir, if they have an Estate,
Or else to bear their Names: So, for by ends,
They take a Wife, and satisfie their friends,
Who are desirous that it should be do,
And for that end, perhaps, Estates bestow;

Which,

Which, when possess'd, is spent another way;
The Spurious Issue do the right betray,
And with their Mother-Strumpets are maintain'd;
The Wife and Children by neglect disdain'd,
Wretched and poor unto their Friends return,
Having got nothing, unless cause to mourn.
The Dire Effects of Lust I cannot tell,
For I suppose its Catalogue's in Hell;
And he perhaps at last may read it there,
Written in flames, fierce as his own whilst here.
I could say more, but yet not half that's done
By these strange Creatures, nor is there scarce one
Of these inhumane Beasts that do not die
As bad as *Bewley's* Pox turns Leprosie,
And Men do catch it by meer phantasie.
Tho' they are chast and honest, yet it doth
Pursue them, and some company on oath
They have been in, and their infected breath
Gave them that Plague, which hast'neth their death,
Or else 'tis Scurvy, or some new disease,
As the base wretch or vain Physician please,
And then a sum of Money must be gave
For to keep corruption from the grave;
And then 'tis doubled, for to hide the cheat:
(O the sad Horrour of debaucht deceit!)
The Body and Estate together go.
And then the only Objects here below,
On which he doth his charity bestow,
Are Whores and Quacks, and perhaps Pages too
Must have a share, or else they will reveal
That which Money doth make them conceal.

Sure trusty Stewards of extensive heaven,
When what's for common good is only given
Unto peculiar friends of theirs, who be
Slaves to their lust, friending debauchery;
These are partakers of as great a fate
As those whose boldness turns them reprobate,
And tho' a Hypocrite doth seem to be
A greater sharer of Morality,
Yet methinks they almost seem all one,
One hides, and t'other tells what he hath done;
But if one Devil's better than another,
Than one of these is better than the t'other:
Hypocrisie preheminence should have,
(Tho' it ha'nt got the priviledge to save)
Because the Reprobate's example may,
By open Custom, make the rugged way
Seem more smooth, and a common sin
Look more pardonable, and so by him
More take example, 'tis he strives to win.
Mad Souls, to fill up Hell! But should there be
Nothing e're acted but Hypocrisie,
Yet Man would be as wicked as he is,
And be no nearer to eternal bliss;
For he who's so unsteady, as to take
Example by such Men, should never make
Me to believe, that he was really chast,
And, without pattern, never had imbrac't:
Such kind of sins at best such virtues weak,
That with such a slender stress will break,
And that's no virtue which cannot withstand
A slight temptation at the second hand:

But

But I believe one might as narrowly pry
For't, as the *Grecian* did for honesty,
And yet find none; and then if Women be
Averse to't too, sure all's iniquity
On this side Heaven, and it with Justice went
Up thither, 'cause here is found no content,
But did regardless and neglected ly,
And with an awful distance was past by.
Instead of hiding their prodigious Acts,
They do reveal, brag of their horrid Facts;
Unless it be some few who hide them, 'cause
They would not seem to violate those laws
Which with their tongues they'r forc'd for to main-
Being grave Counsellers or Aldermen,　　　(tain,
Or else the Wives Relations are alive,
And then, if known, some other way they'l drive
Their golden wheels, that way doth seem uneven,
Then the Estate most certainly is given
Some other way, or else 'tis setled so
As he may never have it to bestow,
Upon his Lusts, therefore he doth seem
For to have a very great esteem
For his pretended Joy; but when her friends
Are dead, then he his cursed life defends,
With what they leave; then the unhappy wife,
With her dear children, lead an horrid life,
And the Estate's put to another use,
And their great kindness turn'd an abuse;
And should I strive their falshood to relate,
Then I should have but *Sisiphus* his fate,

　　　　　　　D　　　　　　　　　　For

For Man is so inconstant and untrue,
He's like a shadow which one doth pursue,
Still flies from's word, nay and perfidious too.
An Instance too of Infidelity
We have in *Egypt*'s false King *Ptolomy*,
Who, tho' he under obligations were,
For to protect *Pompey* from the snare,
Who fled to him for succour, yet base he
Did command his death most treacherously;
He was inconstant too, or else design'd
The same at first, so alter'd words not mind,
Which is much worse, for when that one doth speak
With a full resolution, for to break
One's word and oath, surely it must be
A greater crime than an inconstancy,
Which is as great failing in the soul
As any sin that reason doth controul,
But I designed for to be short, so must
Be sure for to keep firm unto the first
That I resolved, or else should reprove
These faults which first I ought for to remove;
Therefore, with *Brutus*, I this point will end,
Who, tho' he ought to have been *Cæsar*'s friend,
By being declared his Heir, yet it was he
Was the first actor in his tragedy:
Perfidious and ungrateful and untrue
He was at once, nay and disloyal too:
A thousand Instances there might be brought,
(Not far fetch'd, tho' they were dearly bought)

To

To prove that Man more false than Woman is,
More unconstant, nay and more perfidious:
But these are Crimes which hell, (I'm sure not hea-
As they pretend, hath peculiar given   ven)
Unto our Sex, but 'tis as false as they,
And that's more false than any one can say.
All Pride and Lust too to our charge they lay,
As if in sin we all were so sublime
As to monopolize each hainous crime;
Nay, Woman now is made the Scape-goat, and
'Tis she must bear sins of all the land:
But I believe there's not a Priest that can
Make an atonement for one single man,
Nay, it is well if he himself can bring
An humble, pious heart for th' offering;
A thing which ought to be inseparable
To men o'th' Gown and of the Sacred Table;
Yet it is sometimes wanting, and they be
Too often sharers of Impiety:
But howsoever the strange World now thrives,
I must not look in my Teachers lives,
But methinks the World doth seem to be
Nought but confusion and degeneracy,
Each Man's so eager of each fatal sin,
As if he fear'd he should not do't again;
Yet still his soul is black, he is the same
At all times, tho' he doth not act all flame,
Because he opportunity doth want,
And to him always there's not a grant

Of

Of Objects for to exercise his will,
And for to shew his great and mighty skill
In all Sciences diabolical,
But when he meets with those which we do call
Base and unjust, why then his part he acts
Most willingly, and then with hell contracts
To do the next thing that they should require;
And being thus inflamed with hellish fire,
He doth to any thing it doth desire,
Unless 'twere possible for hell to say,
They should be good, for then they'd disobey.
I am not sorry you do Females hate,
But rather reckon we're more fortunate,
Because I find, when you'r right understood,
You are at enmity with all that's good,
And should you love them, I should think they were
A growing bad, but still keep as you are:
I need not bid you, for you must I'm sure,
And in your present wretched state indure;
'Tis an impossible you should be true,
As for a Woman to act like to you,
Which I am sure will not accomplish'd be,
Till heaven's turn'd hell, and that's repugnancy;
And when vice is virtue you shall have
A share of that which makes most Females brave,
Which transmutations I am sure can't be;
So thou must lie in vast eternity,
With prospect of thy endless misery,
When Woman, your imagin'd Fiend, shall live
Bless'd with the Joys that Heaven can always give.

F I N I S.

THE Female Advocate: OR, AN ANSWER TO A LATE SATYR Against the Pride, Lust and Inconstancy OF WOMAN. *Written by a Lady in Vindication of her Sex.* (1707; ESTC T191079 is reproduced, by permission of the University of Leeds Library (shelfmark Brotherton Collection LT EGE). The text block of the title page measures 160 × 90 mm. The text block of 'To the Reader' measures 154 × 90 mm.

Words or passages which are difficult to read:

8.13:   But were he true, none serve him as they shou'd

THE
Female Advocate:
OR, AN
ANSWER
TO A LATE
SATYR
Against the
Pride, Lust and Inconstancy
OF
WOMAN.

Written by a Lady in Vindication of her Sex.

LONDON:
Printed For *J. Taylor*, at the *Ship* in St. *Paul*'s Church-Yard. 1707.

TO THE READER.

THAT which makes many Books come come abroad into the World without Prefaces, is the only reason that incites me to one, viz. the smallness of them; being willing to let my Reader know why this is so: For as one great Commendation of our Sex, is to know much, and speak little, so an Intelligent Modesty informs my Soul, I ought to put a Period to the intended Length of the insuing Lines, lest censuring Criticks should measure my Tongue by my Pen, and condemn me for a Talkative by the Length of my Poem. Tho' I confess the Illustrious Subject requires (nay commands) an Enlargement from any other

The Preface.

Pen than mine, (or those under the same Circumstances;) but I think it is good Frugality for young Beginners to send forth a small Venture at first, and see how that passes the merciless Ocean of Criticks, and what Returns it makes, and so accordingly adventure the next time. I might, if I pleas'd, make an Excuse for the Publication of my Book, as many others do; but then, perhaps, the World might think 'twas only a feign'd Unwillingness: But when I found I could not hinder the Publication, I set a resolution to bear patiently the Censures of the World, for I expected its Severity, the first Copy being so ill writ, and so much blotted, that it could scarce be read; and they that had the Charge of it, in the room of Blots, writ what they pleas'd, and much different from my Intention. I find the main Objection is, That I should Answer so rude a Book, when, if it had not been against our Sex, I should not have Read it, much less have Answer'd it; but I think its being so required the sharper Answer, and severer Contradictions. I suppose some will think the Alterations occasion'd by their dislike

The Preface.

of the former: If that had been intended for the Press, some things there inserted, had been left out; which I have now done, tho' they might pass well enough in Private, they were not fit to be exposed to every Eye; but I think, when a Man is so extravagant as to Damn all Womankind for the Crimes of a few, he ought to be corrected: But in his Second Edition he hath been more favourable, yet there he goes beyond the bounds of Modesty and Civility, and exclaims not only against Vertue, but moral Honesty too, and supposes he hath banish'd all Goodness out of them; but it will be an impossible thing, because they are more essentially Good than Men; for 'tis observed in all Religions, that Women are the truest Devotionists, and the most Pious, and more Heavenly than those who pretend to be the most perfect and rational Creatures; for many Men, with Conceit of their own Perfections, neglect that which should make them so; as some mistaken Persons, who think if they are of the right Church they shall be infallibly saved, when they never follow the Rules that lead to Salvation: And when Persons with this Inscription pass currant

The Preface.

rant in *Heaven*, then should it be according to my *Antagonist's* Fancy, that all *Men* are good, and fitting for *Heaven*, because they are *Men*; and *Women* irreversibly *Damn'd*, because they are *Women*: But that *Heaven* should make a *Male* and *Female* both of the same *Species*, both indued with the like rational *Souls*, for two such differing Ends, is the most notorious Principle, and the most unlikely of any that ever was maintain'd by any rational *Man*; and I shall never take it for an Article of my Faith, being assured that *Heaven* is for all those whose Purity and Obedience to its Law, qualifies them for it, whether *Male* or *Female*; *to which Place the latter seem to have the justest Claim, is the Opinion of one of its Votaries.*

S. F.

THE
Female Advocate,
OR,
An Answer to a late Satyr against the Pride, Lust and Inconstancy, &c. of Woman.

BLasphemous Wretch! How canst thou think or say
Some Curst or Banisht Fiend Usurpt the Sway
When *Eve* was Form'd? For then's deny'd by you
God's Omnipresence and Omniscience too:
Without which Attributes he could not be
The greatest and supreamest Deity:
Nor can Heav'n sleep, tho' it may mourn to see
Degen'rate Man speak such vile Blasphemy.

When from dark *Chaos* Heav'n the World did make,
And all was Glorious it did undertake;
Then

Then were in *Eden*'s Garden freely plac'd
Each thing that's pleasant to the Sight or Taste,
'Twas fill'd with *Beasts* and *Birds*, *Trees* hung with Fruit,
That might with Man's Celestial Nature suit:
The World being made thus spacious and compleat,
Then Man was form'd, who seemed nobly Great.
When Heav'n survey'd the Works that it had done,
Saw Male and Female, but found Man alone,
A barren Sex, and insignificant,
Then Heav'n made Woman to supply the want,
And to make perfect what before was scant:
Surely then she a Noble Creature is,
Whom Heav'n thus made to consummate all Bliss.
Tho' Man had Being first, yet methinks She
In Nature shou'd have the Supremacy;
For Man was form'd out of dull senceless Earth,
But Woman had a much more Noble Birth:
For when the Dust was purify'd by Heaven,
Made into Man, and Life unto it given,
Then the Almighty and All-wise God said,
That Woman of that Species shou'd be made;
Which was no sooner said, but it was done,
'Cause 'twas not fit for Man to be alone.

Thus have I prov'd Woman's Creation good,
And not inferior, when right understood,
To that of Man's; for both one Maker had,
Which made all good; then how cou'd *Eve* be bad?

But

The Female Advocate.

But then you'll say, tho' she at first was pure,
Yet in that State she did not long endure.
'Tis true; but yet her Fall examine right,
We find most Men have banish'd Truth for spight:
Nor is she quite so guilty as some make,
For *Adam* most did of the Guilt partake;
While he from God's own Mouth had the Com-
But Woman had it at the second hand: (mand,
The Devil's Strength weak Woman might deceive,
But *Adam* only tempted was by *Eve*:
She had the strongest Tempter, and least Charge;
Man's knowing most, doth make his Sin more
But tho' that Woman Man to Sin did lead, (large.
Yet since her Seed hath bruis'd the Serpent's Head,
Why should she thus be made a publick scorn,
Of whom the Great Almighty God was born?
Surely to speak one slighting word, must be
A kind of murmuring Impiety:
But yet their greatest Haters still prove such
Who formerly have loved them too much;
And from the Proverb they are not exempt,
Too much familiarity has bred Contempt.
And as in *Adam* all Mankind did die,
They make all Base for one's Immodesty;
Nay, make the Name a kind of Magick Spell,
As if 'twould Conjure married Men to Hell.

Woman! By Heaven, the very Name's a Charm,
And will my Verse against all Criticks arm.

The Female Advocate.

The *Muses* or *Apollo* doth inspire
Heroick Poets; but yours is a Fire
Pluto from Hell did send by *Incubus*,
Because we make their Hell less populous,
Or else you ne'er had damn'd the Females thus:
But if so universally they are
Dispos'd to Mischief, what need you declare
Peculiar Faults? when all the World might see
With each approaching Morn a Prodigy.
Man curse bad Woman! I cou'd hear as well
The black infernal Devils curse their Hell;
When there had been no such damn'd Place we know,
If they themselves had not first made it so.
In Lust perhaps you others have excell'd,
And made all Whores that possibly wou'd yield;
And courted all the Females in your way,
Then did design at last to make a Prey
Of some pure Virgins; or what's almost worse,
Make some chaste Wives to merit a Divorce:
But 'cause they hated your insatiate Mind,
Therefore you call what's Vertuous, Unkind;
And disappointments did your Soul perplex,
So in meer spight you curse the Female Sex.
I would not judge you thus, only I find
You wou'd adulterate all Womankind,
Not only with your Pen; you higher soar,
You'd exclude Marriage, make the World a Whore.

But if all Men shou'd of your Humour be,
And shou'd rob *Hymen* of his Deity,
They soon wou'd find the Inconveniency.
Then hostile Spirits would be forc'd to Peace,
Because the World so slowly wou'd increase.
They wou'd be glad to keep their Men at home,
And ev'ry King want more t' attend his Throne:
Nay, shou'd an *English* Prince resolve that he
Wou'd keep the number of's Nobility;
And this dull Custom some few years maintain'd,
There wou'd be none less than a Peer i'th' Land;
And I do fancy 'twou'd be pretty sport,
To see a Kingdom cram'd into a Court.
Sure a strange World, when one shall nothing see,
Unless a Bawdy-house or Nunnery.
For shou'd this Act e'er pass, Woman wou'd fly
Unto dark Caves to save her Chastity.
She only in a Marriage-Bed delights,
The very Name of *Whore* her Soul affrights:
And when that Sacred Ceremony's gone,
Woman I'm sure will chuse to live alone.

There's none can number all those vertuous
    Dames
Which chose cold death before their Lovers flames.
The chaste *Lucretia*, whom proud *Tarquin* lov'd,
Her self she slew: Her Chastity she prov'd.
But I've gone further than I need have done,
Since we have got Examples nearer home:

Witness those *Saxon* Ladies who did fear
The loss of Honour when the *Danes* were here;
And cut their Lips and Noses, that they might
Not pleasing seem, or give the *Danes* delight:
Thus having done what they cou'd justly do,
At last they fell their Sacrifices too.
I cou'd say more, but History will tell
Many Examples that do these excel.

   In Constancy they often Men excel.
That steady Vertue in their Souls do dwell;
She's not so fickle and frail as Men pretend,
But can keep constant to a faithful Friend;
And tho' Man's always alt'ring of his mind,
He says, Inconstancy's in Womankind;
And would persuade us that we engross all
That's either fickle, vain, or whimsical.
Man's fancy'd Truth small Vertue doth express;
Our's is Constancy, their's is Stubbornness.
In faithful Love our Sex do them out-shine,
And is more constant than the Masculine:
For where is there that Husband that e'er dy'd,
Or ever suffer'd with his loving Bride?
But num'rous trains of chast Wives oft expire
With their dear Husbands, wrapt in flaming fire;
We'd to the same if Custom did require.
But this is done by *Indian* Women, who
Do make their Constancy immortal too,
As is their Fame; while happy *India* yields
More glorious *Phœnix* than th' *Arabian* Fields.

The Female Advocate.

The *German* Women Constancy did show
When *Wensberg* was Besieg'd, begg'd they might go
Out of the City, with no bigger Packs
Than each of them cou'd carry on their Backs.
The wond'ring World expected they'd have gone
Laded with Treasures from their Native home;
But crossing expectation, each did take
Her Husband, as her burden on her back;
So sav'd him from intended Death, and she
At once gave him both Life and Liberty.
How many loving Wives have often dy'd
Thro' extreme Grief by their cold Husbands side?
If this ben't Constancy, why then the Sun
Or Earth do not a constant progress run.

There's thousands of Examples that will prove
Woman is true and constant in chast Love:
But when to us pretended Love is made,
We yielding, find it Lust in Masquerade:
Then we disown it, Vertue says we must,
We well may change, I think the reason just.
Change did I say, that word I must forbear,
No, she, bright Star, won't wander from her sphere
Of Vertue (in which Female Souls do move)
Nor will she joyn with an insatiate Love;
For she that's first espous'd to Vertue, must
Be most Inconstant when she yields to Lust.

But now the Scene is alter'd, and those who
Were esteem'd Modest by a blush or two,

Are

Are represented quite another way,
Worse than Mock-verse doth the most solid Play.
She that takes pious Precepts for her Rule,
Is thought, by some, a kind of ill-bred Fool;
They wou'd have all bred up in *Venus*-School.
And if that by her speech or carriage, she
Doth seem to have sence of a Deity,
She straight is taxt with ungentility:
Unless it be the little blinded Boy,
Cupid, that childish God, that trifling Toy;
That certain nothing, whom they feign to be
The Sun of *Venus*, Daughter to the Sea.
But were he true, none serve him as they shou'd,
For commonly those who adore this God,
Do't only in a melancholy mood;
Or else a sort of Hypocrites they are,
Who invocate him only as a snare:
And by him they do sacred Love pretend,
Whenas, Heav'n knows, they have a baser end.

Nor is he God of Love; but if I must
Give him a title, He's the God of Lust.
And surely Woman impious must be,
Whene'er she doth become his Votary;
Unless she will believe without controul,
Those that did hold a Woman had no Soul;
And then doth think no obligation lies
On her to act what may be just or wise:
And only strive to please her Appetite,
And to imbrace that which doth most delight.

And

The Female Advocate.

And when she doth this Paradox believe,
Whatever Faith doth please she may receive.
She may be Turk, Jew, Atheist, Infidel,
Or any thing, 'cause she need fear no Hell;
For if she hath no Soul, what need she fear
Something, she knows not what, or when, or where?

But hold, I think I should be silent now,
Because a Woman's Soul you do allow.
But had we none, you'd say we had, else you
Cou'd never Damn us at the rate you do.
What, dost thou think thou hast a priv'lege given,
That those whom thou dost bless, shall mount to
And those thou cursest, unto Hell must go? (heaven?
And so dost think to fill th' *Abyss* below
Quite full of Females, hoping there may be
No room for Souls as big with Vice as thee.
But if that thou with such vain hopes should'st die,
I'th' fluid Air thou must not think to fly;
Or enter into Heav'n, thy weight of Sin
Wou'd crush the Damn'd, and so thoud'st enter in.

But hold, I am uncharitable here,
Thou may'st repent, tho' that's a thing I fear.
But if thou shou'd'st repent, why then again,
It would, at best, but mitigate thy pain;
Because thou hast been vile to that degree,
That thy repentance must eternal be.
For wer't thou guilty of no other Crime
Than what thou lately puttest into Rhime,

Why

Why that, were there no more Offences given,
Were crime enough to shut the gate of Heav'n:
But, put together all that thou dost do,
It will not only shut, but barr it too.

When wise Heav'n made Woman, it design'd
Her for the charming object of Mankind:
And surely Man degenerate must be,
That doth deny our Native purity.
Nor is there scarce a thing that can be worse,
Than turning of a Blessing to a Curse.
'Tis to make Heav'n mistaken when you say
It meant at first, what proves another way:
For Woman was created good, and she
Was thought the best of frail of Mortality:
An help for Man, his greatest good on Earth,
Made for to sympathize his Grief and Mirth;
Then why shou'd Man pretend she's worse than hell,
The only plague o'th World, and in her dwell (
All that is base or ill? no, she's not so,
Rather she is the greatest good below;
Most real vertue and true happiness,
His only steady and most constant bliss.

I must confess there are some bad, and they,
Lead by an *Ignis fatuus*, go astray;
All are not forc'd to wander in false way:
Only some few whose dark benighted sence,
For want of light, han't power to make defence

Against

Against those many tempting pleasures, which
Not only theirs, but Masculine Souls bewitch.
But you'd persuade us that 'tis we alone
Are guilty of all Crimes, and you have none,
Unless some few, which you call Fools, (who be
Espous'd to Wives, and live in Chastity)
But the most Rational, without which we
Doubtless shou'd question your Humanity;
And I wou'd praise them more, only I fear,
If I shou'd do it, 'twou'd make me appear
Unto the World much fonder than I be
Of that same State, for I love Liberty.
Nor do I think there's a necessity
For all to enter Beds, like *Noah*'s Beast
Into his Ark; I would have some releast
From the dear cares of that same lawful State;
But I'll not dictate, I'll leave all to Fate.
Yet do I think a single life is best
For those that love to contemplate at rest:
For then they're free from trifling Toys, and may
Uninterrupted Nature's works survey.

   Had my Antagonist but spent his time
Making true Verse instead of spightful Rhime,
As a small Poet, he had gain'd some Praise,
But now his Malice blasts his twig of Bays.
I do not wish you had, for I believe
It is impossible for to deceive
Any with what you write, because that you
Do only insert things supposed true:

And if by suppoſition I may go,
Then I'll ſuppoſe all Men are wicked too,
Since I am ſure there are ſo many ſo.
And 'cauſe you have made *Whores* of all you cou'd,
So, if you durſt, you'd ſay all Women wou'd;
Which words do only argue guilt and ſpight:
All makes you cheap in ev'ry Mortals ſight.
And it doth ſhew that you have always been
Only with Women guilty of that Sin.
You ne'er deſir'd, nor were you fit for thoſe,
Whoſe modeſt carriage doth their minds diſcloſe:
And, Sir, methinks you do deſcribe ſo well
The way and manner *Bewley* enter'd Hell,
As if your love for her had made you go
Down to the black infernal ſhades below.

 But I ſuppoſe you never was ſo near,
Nay, if you had, you ſcarce would have been here,
For had they ſeen you, they had kept you there;
Unleſs they thought, whene'er it was you came,
Your red-hot entrance might encreaſe the flame
(If burning Hell add to their extreme pain)
And ſo were glad to turn you off again.

 There's one thing more I do believe beſide
Might be occaſion'd by their haughty Pride;
They knew you Rival'd them in all their Crimes,
Wherewith they could debauch the willing times.
And as fond Mortals hate a Rival, they
Loving their Pride, were loth to let you ſtay,

For

The Female Advocate.

For fear that you might their black deeds excel,
Ufurp their Seat, and be the Prince of Hell.
But I believe that you will let your Hate
O'er-rule your Pride, and you'll not wifh the State
Of Governing, becaufe your deceiv'd mind
Perfuades, your Subjects will be Womenkind.
But I believe, whenever comes the tryal,
Ask but for Ten, and you'll have a denial.
You'd think your felf far happier than you be,
Were you but half fo fure of Heaven as we.
But when you are in Hell if you fhou'd find
More than I fpeak of, then think Heaven defign'd
Them for a part of your Eternal Fate,
Becaufe they're things which you fo much do
But why you fhould do fo I cannot tell, (hate.
Unlefs 'tis what makes you in love with Hell:
And having fallen-out with Goodnefs, you
Muft have Antipathy 'gainft Woman too.
For Virtue and they fo nearly are ally'd
That none their mutual tyes can e'er divide.
Like Light and Heat, incorporate they are,
And interwove with providential Care.
But I'm too dull to give my Sex due Praife,
The task befits a Laureat Crown'd with Bays:
And yet all he can fay will be but fmall,
A Copy differs from th' Original.
For fhould he fleep under *Parnaſſus* Hill,
Implore the Mufes for to guide his Quill,
And fhou'd they help him, yet his Praife wou'd
At beft but undervalluing difefteem. (feem

For he wou'd come so short of what they are
His lines won't with one single Act compare,
But to say truest, is to say, that she
Is Good and Vertuous unto that degree
As you pretend she's Bad, and that's beyond
Imagination, 'cause you set no bound:
And then one certain definition is
To say that she doth comprehend all Bliss.
And that she's all that's pious, chast and true,
Heroick, constant, nay and modest too:
The later Vertue is a thing you doubt,
But 'tis cause you ne'er sought to find it out.
You question where there's such a thing or no,
'Tis only 'cause you hope you've lost a foe,
A hated object, yet a stranger too.
I'll speak like you, if such a thing there be,
I'm certain that she doth not dwell with thee.
Thou art *Antipodes* to that, and all
That's Good, or that we simply Civil call.
From Vertue's yoke thou hast thy self releast,
Turn'd Bully, Hector, and a human Beast.
That Beasts do speak, it rarely comes to pass,
Yet you may paralel with *Balaam*'s Ass.
You do describe a Woman so, that one
Would almost think she had the Fiends out-done:
As if at her strange Birth did shine no Star,
Or Planet, only Furies in Conjunction were;
And did conspire what mischief they shou'd do,
Each act his part, and her with plagues pursue,
'Tis false in her, yet 'tis summ'd up in you.

You

You almost wou'd perswade one that you thought
That Providence to a low ebb was brought;
And that to *Eve* and *Jezebel* was given
Souls of so great extent, that Heav'n was driven
Into a straight, and liberality
Had made her void of wanting, to supply
These latter bodies, she was forc'd to take
Their souls asunder, and so numbers make,
And transmigrate them into others, and
Still shift them as she finds the matter stand.
'Tis 'cause they are the worst makes me believe
You must imagine *Jezebel* and *Eve*.
But I'm no *Pythagorean*, to conclude
One Soul could serve for *Abraham* and *Jude*:
Or think that Heaven's so Bankrupt, or so Poor,
But that each Body has one Soul or more.
I do not find our Sex so near ally'd,
Either in Disobedience or in Pride,
Unto the 'bove-nam'd Females (for I'm sure
They are refin'd, or else were always pure)
That I must needs conceit their Souls the same,
Tho' I confess there's some that merit blame:
But yet their faults only thus much infer,
That we're not made so perfect, but may err;
Which adds much Lustre to a Vertuous mind,
And 'tis her Prudence makes her Soul confin'd
Within the bounds of Goodness, for if she
Was all Perfection unto that degree,
That 'twas impossible to do amiss,
Then Heaven, not she, must have the praise of this.

But

But she's in such a state as she may fall,
And, without care, her freedom may inthral.
But to keep pure and free in such a case,
Argues each Vertue with its proper grace.
And as a Woman's composition is
Most soft and gentle, she has happiness
In that her Soul is of that nature too,
And yields to any thing that Heav'n will do;
Takes an Impression when 'tis Seal'd in Heaven,
Turns to a cold refusal, when 'tis given
By any other hand: She's all divine,
And by a splendid Lustre doth out-shine
All masculine Souls, who only seem to be
Made up of Pride and their lov'd Luxury.
So great is Man's Ambition that he would
Have all the Wealth and Power if he could,
That is bestow'd upon the several Thrones
Of the World's Monarchs, covets all their Crowns.
And by Experience it hath been found
The word Ambition's not an empty sound.
There's not an History which doth not shew
Man's pride, ambition and his falshood too.
For if at any time th'ambitious have
Least shew of Honour, then their Souls grow brave,
Grow big and restless, they are not at ease,
'Till they have a more fatal way to please,
Look fair and true, when falsely they intend;
So from low Subject, grow a Monarch's Friend.
And by grave Councels they their good pretend,
When 'tis guilt Poyson and oft works their end.

The

The Son who must succeed, is too much lov'd,
Must be pull'd down (his Councel is approv'd)
For fear he willingly should grow too great,
Desire to rule, should mount his Father's Seat.
So he's dispatch'd, and then all those that be
Next in the way are his adherency:
And then, the better to secure the State,
It is but just they shou'd receive his Fate.
So by degrees he for himself makes room,
His Prince is streightway shut up in his Tomb,
And then the false Usurper mounts the Throne.
Or would do so at least, but commonly
He ne're sits firm, but with revenge doth die,
But, thank Heav'n, there's but few that reach so high,
For the known crimes makes a wise Prince take care.
And thus by what I've said, we plainly find
That Men more impious are than Womankind.
So those who by their abject fortunes are
Remote from Courts no less their pride declare,
In being uneasie and envying all who be
In State above them, or Priority.
But 'tis impossible for to relate
Their boundless pride, or their prodigious hate,
To all that fortune hath but smil'd upon,
In a degree that is above their own,
And thou, proud fool, that vertue would'st subdue,
Envying all good, do'st towre o're Woman too,
Which doth betray a base ignoble Mind,
And speaks thee nothing but a blustring Wind.

But

But in so great a Lab'rinth as man's pride,
I should not enter, nor won't be imploy'd,
For to search out their strange and unknown
So many are apparent in those times, (crimes,
My dull Arithmetick can never tell
Half of the Sins that commonly do dwell
In one poor sordid Swain, then how can I
Define the Court's or Town's Debauchery!
Their pride in some small measure I have shown,
But 'tis too great a Task for me alone;
Nor yet more possible I shou'd repeat
The Crimes of Men extravagantly great;
I wou'd not name them, but to let them see
I know they're bad and odious unto me.
'Tis true, pride makes Men great in their own eyes,
But them proportionable I despise;
And tho' Ambition still aims to be high,
Yet Lust, at best, is but Beastiality;
A Sin with which there's none that can compare,
Not Pride nor Envy, &c. for this doth insnare
Not only those whom it at first inflam'd,
This Sin must have a Part'ner to be sham'd,
And punish'd like himself. Hold, one won't do,
He must have more, for he doth still pursue
The Agents of his Passion; 'tis not Wife,
That mutual Name, can regulate his Life,
And tho' he for his Lust might have a shrow'd,
And there might be *Polygamy* allow'd,
Yet all his Wives wou'd surely be abhorr'd,
And still some common *Lais* be ador'd.

Most

Most mortally the Name of Wife they hate,
Yet they will take one as their proper fate,
That they may have a Child legitimate,
To be their Heir, if they have an Estate,
Or else to bear their Names: So for by ends,
They take a Wife, and satisfie their Friends;
Who are desirous that it should be so,
And for that end, perhaps, Estates bestow;
Which, when possess'd, is spent another way;
The spurious Issue do the right betray,
And with their Mother-Strumpets are maintain'd;
The Wife and Children by neglect disdain'd,
Wretched and poor, unto their Friends return,
Having got nothing, unless cause to mourn.
The dire Effects of Lust I cannot tell,
But I suppose they're Catalogu'd in Hell;
And he, perhaps, at last may read it there,
Written in flames, fierce as his own whilst here,
I could say more, but yet not half that's done
By these strange Creatures, nor is there scarce one
Of these inhumane Beasts that does not die
As bad as *Bewley*'s Pox turns Leprosie,
And Men do catch it by meer phantasie.
Tho' they seem chast and honest, yet it doth
Pursue them, while they swear it with an oath
'Twas only in Company, infected breath
Gave them that *Plague*, which hastens on their
Or else the Scurvy, or some new Disease, (death,
As the base Wretch, or vain Physician please;

D   Them

Then a round sum the Surgeon he must have,
To keep Corruption from the threatning grave;
And then 'tis doubled, for to hide the cheat;
(O the sad horrour of debaucht Deceit!)
The Body and Estate together go,
And then the only objects here below,
On which he doth his Charity bestow,
Are Whores and Quacks, and perhaps Pages too
Must have a share, or else they will reveal
What Money doth oblige 'em to conceal.
Sure trusty Stewards of extensive Heaven,
When what's for common good is only given
Unto peculiar friends of theirs, who be
Slaves to their lust, friending debauchery;
These are partakers of as great a fate
As those whose boldness turns them reprobate,
And tho' a Hyprocrite doth seem to be
A greater sharer of Morality,
And yet methinks they almost seem all one,
One hides, and t'other tells what he hath done;
But if one Devil's better than another,
Then one of these is better than the t'other:
Hypocrisie preheminence should have,
(Tho' it has not the privilege to save)
Because the Reprobate's example may,
By open Custom, make the rugged way
Seem much more smooth, and a vile common sin
More pardonable look, and so by him
More take example: 'tis he strives to win

Mad

Mad Souls, to fill up Hell! But should there be
Nothing e're acted but Hypocrisie,
Yet Man would be as wicked as he is,
And be no nearer to eternal bliss;
For he who's so unsteady, as to take
Example by such Men, should never make
Me to believe that he was really chast,
And, without pattern, never had imbrac't:
Such kind of force at best, such virtue's weak,
That streight with such a slender stress will break;
And that's no virtue which cannot withstand
A slight temptation at the second hand:
But I believe one might as deeply pry
For't, as the *Grecian* did for honesty,
And yet find none; and then if Women be
Averse to't too, sure all's iniquity
On this side Heaven, and it with Justice went
Up thither, 'cause here is found no content,
But did regardless and neglected ly,
And with an awful distance was past by.
Instead of hiding their prodigious Acts,
They do reveal, brag of their horrid Facts;
Unless it be some few who hide them, 'cause
They would not seem to violate those laws
Which with their tongues they'r forc'd for to main-
Being grave Counsellors or Aldermen, (tain,
Or else the Wives Relations are alive,
And then, if known, some other way they'll drive
Their golden wheels, that way doth seem uneven,
Then the Estate most certainly is given

Some other way, or elſe 'tis ſetled ſo
As he may never have it to beſtow
Upon his Luſts, and therefore he doth ſeem
To have a very high and great eſteem
For his pretended Joy; but when her friends
Are dead, then he his curſed life defends,
With what they leave; then the unhappy wife,
With her dear children, lead an horrid life,
And the Eſtate's put to another uſe,
And their great kindneſs turn'd to an abuſe;
And ſhould I ſtrive their falſhood to relate,
Then I ſhould have but *Siſiphus* his fate,
For Man is ſo inconſtant and untrue,
He's like a ſhadow which one doth purſue,
Still flies from's word, nay and perfidious too.
An Inſtance too of Infidelity
We have in *Egypt*'s falſe King *Ptolomy*,
Who, tho' he under obligations were,
To ſecure luckleſs *Pompey* from the ſnare,
Who fled to him for ſuccour, yet baſe he
Approv'd his Death, and Murderer let go free;
He was inconſtant too, or elſe deſign'd
The ſame at firſt, ſo alter'd words not mind,
Which is much worſe, for when that one doth ſpeak
With a full reſolution for to break
One's word and oath, moſt ſurely it muſt be
A greater crime than an inconſtancy;
Which is as great a failing in the ſoul
As any ſin that reaſon doth controul.
But I deſigned to be ſhort, ſo muſt
Be ſure to keep confin'd to what I firſt

Reſolved

Resolved on, or else I should reprove
These faults which first I ought for to remove;
Therefore, with *Brutus*, I this point will end,
Who, tho' he ought to have been *Cæsar*'s friend,
By being declar'd his Heir, yet it was he
Was the first actor in his Tragedy:
Perfidious, and ungrateful, and untrue
He was at once, nay and disloyal too:
A thousand Instances there might be brought,
(Not far fetch'd neither, tho' more dearly brought)
To prove that Man more false than Woman is,
Far more unconstant, nay perfidious:
But these are Crimes which hell, (I'm sure not hea-
As they pretend, hath in peculiar given   ven)
Unto our Sex, but that's as false as they,
And that's more false than any one can say.
All Pride and Lust too to our charge they lay,
As if in Sin we all were so sublime
As to Monopolize each hainous Crime;
Nay, Woman now is made the Scape-goat, and
'Tis she must bear the Sins of all the Land:
But I believe there's not a Priest that can
Make an Atonement for one single Man;
Nay, it is well if he himself can bring
An humble, pious Heart for th' Offering;
A thing which ought to be inseparable
To Men o'th' Gown and of the Sacred Table;
Yet it is sometimes wanting, and they be
Too often sharers of Impiety:
But howsoever the strange World now thrives,
I must not look into my Teachers lives,

But

But now methinks the World doth seem to be
Nought but Confusion and Degeneracy:
Each Man's so eager of each fatal Sin,
As if he fear'd he should not do't again;
Yet still his Soul is black, he is the same
At all times, tho' he doth not act all flame,
Because he opportunity doth want,
And to him always there is not a grant
Of Objects for to exercise his will,
And for to shew his great and mighty skill
In Sciences all diabolical.
But when he meets with those which we do call
Base and unjust, why then his part he acts
Most willingly, and then with Hell contracts
To do the next thing that they should require;
And being thus inflam'd with hellish fire,
He yields to any thing it doth desire;
Unless 'twere possible for hell to say,
They should be good, for then they'd disobey.
I am not sorry you do Females hate,
But rather deem our selves more fortunate,
Because I find, when you're right understood,
You are at enmity with all that's good;
And should you love them, I should think they
A growing bad, but still keep as yon are. (were
I need not bid you, for you must I'm sure,
And in your present wretched state indure;
'Tis as impossible you should be true,
As for a Woman to act like to you;
Which I am sure will not accomplish'd be,
Till Heaven's turn'd Hell, and that's repugnancy;
When

The Female Advocate.

When Vice turns Vertue, then 'tis you shall have
A share of that which makes most Females brave,
Which transmutations I am sure can't be;
So thou must lie in vast Eternity,
With prospect of thy endless Misery;
When Woman, your imagin'd Fiend, shall live
Bless'd with the Joys that Heaven can always give.

FINIS.

BOOKS Printed for *J. Taylor*, at the *Ship* in St. *Paul's* Church-Yard.

THE new World of Words: Or, Universal *English* Dictionary. Containing an account of the Original or Proper Sense, and Various Significations of all hard Words derived from other Languages, *viz. Hebrew, Arabick, Syriack, Greek, Latin, Italian, French, Spanish, British, Saxon, Danish, Dutch,* &c. as now made use of in our *English* Tongue. Together with a brief and plain Explication of all Terms relating to any of the Arts and Sciences, either Liberal or Mechanical, *viz. Grammar, Rhetorick, Logick, Theology, Law, Metaphysick, Ethicks, Natural Philosophy, Physick, Surgery, Anatomy, Chymistry, Pharmacy, Botanicks, Arithmetick, Geometry, Astronomy, Astrology, Cosmography, Geography, Hydrography, Navigation, Architecture, Fortification, Dialling, Surveying, Gauging, Opticks, Catoptricks, Dioptricks,*

tricks, *Perspective, Musick, Mechanicks, Staticks, Chiromancy, Physiognomy, Heraldry, Merchandize, Maritime* and *Military Affairs, Agriculture, Gardening, Handicrafts, Jewelling, Painting, Carving, Engraving, Confectionery, Cokery, Horsemanship, Hawking, Hunting, Fowling, Fishing,* &c. To which is added, the Interpretation of Proper Names of Men and Women, that derive their Original from the above mention'd Ancient and Modern Tongues, with those of Writs and Processes at Law: Also the *Greek* and *Latin* Names of divers sorts of *Animals, Plants, Metals, Minerals,* &c. and several other remarkable Matters more particularly express'd in the *Preface.* Compiled by *Edward Phillips,* Gent. The Sixth Edition, Revised, Corrected, and Improved; with the Addition of near Twenty Thousand Words, from the best Authors, Domestick and Foreign, that Treat of several Subjects: By *J. K.* Philobibl. *A Work very necessary for Strangers, as well as our own Country-men, in order to the right understanding of what they Speak, Write, or Read.* Fol.

A Collection of Poems on several Occasions, *viz.* on Friendship, a Satyr against the Muses, on Liberty, repulse to *Alcander,* the Vision, Songs on Love, the Emulation, on the Death of *John Dryden,* Esq; the Extacy, to the Queen, to the Lady *Cambell,* to Mr. *Norris* on his Idea of Happiness, the Power of Love, the Invocation, on the Death of King *William,* on my Wedding Day. To which is added a Pastoral, Entitled, *The Fond Shepherdess.* By Mrs. *Sarah Fyge Egerton.* 8vo.

POEMS ON Several Occasions, Together with a PASTORAL. By Mrs. *S.F.* (1703; ESTC T12548) is reproduced, by permission of the William Andrews Clark Memorial Library (shelfmark PR341. E17. P7*). The text block of the title page measures 174 × 105 mm. The text block of the dedication measures 174 × 110 mm.

Words or passages which are difficult to read, partly because of the tight binding of the original:

1.13:	Or	49.14:	Sure	75.1:	The ecchoing
1.14:	That	49.15:	Those	75.2:	To all
1.15:	Sometimes	49.16:	Thus	75.3:	Till it
1.16:	A soft	49.17:	And	75.6:	Or he
1.17:	Strait	49.18:	I would	75.7:	Each Atom
1.18:	Which	49.19:	But am	75.8:	And flowing
6.10:	Which untamed Beasts	53.3:	And	75.9:	Altho' the
		53.4:	Soft	75.10:	He surely
11.1:	Base	53.5:	Till	77.1:	But oh!
15.9:	And put the Schreiks	53.6:	Husht	77.2:	No more
17.14:	In	53.7:	And all	77.3:	And all
17.15:	Greatness	53.8:	Methoughts	77.8:	Sing their
17.18:	Goodness	53.9:	Whose	83.15:	With passive
43.1:	But	53.10:	Gay	83.16:	For Fate
43.2:	I'm	53.11:	With	83.17:	But her
43.3:	Check	53.12:	I gaz'd	83.18:	Then why
43.4:	As	53.13:	And thought	83.19:	For what
43.5:	My	53.14:	With equal	83.21:	Then live
43.6:	Nor	53.15:	If he	83.22:	Nor grieve
45.1:	I can	53.16:	His Eyes	83.24:	And that
45.2:	Hear	53.17:	As if	83.25:	Those who
45.3:	View	53.18:	A thousand	83.26:	Neglect
45.4:	As	53.19:	For every	95.1:	Methinks
45.5:	Ye	53.20:	His welcome	95.2:	Like him
45.6:	Who's	53.21:	On a soft	95.3:	In his
45.7:	Keep	65.1:	Tho'	95.4:	But you
45.8:	Put	65.2:	Methinks	95.5:	Your Power
45.9:	The	65.3:	The	96.6:	Your own
45.10:	Sound	65.4:	Instead	95.7:	Wit Fortune [sic]
45.11:	Each	65.5:	Need	95.8:	Each with
45.12:	Bud	65.6:	You	95.9:	For the
45.13:	But	65.7:	Then	95.10:	As did
45.14:	In	65.8:	Fatal	95.11:	That bless'd
45.15:	No	65.9:	Your	95.12:	With the
49.11:	Why	65.10:	So far	95.13:	They would
49.12:	Let	65.11:	We	95.14:	But are
49.13:	Not	70.14:	With me	95.15:	Besides they

95.16:	They've	115.1:	We	11.6:	And ev'ry
95.17:	And	115.2:	But	11.7:	Other Youths
95.18:	But	115.3:	Speak	11.8:	As he's
95.19:	For	115.4:	Whether	11.9:	Lost to
95.20:	May	115.6:	My	11.10:	And only
95.21:	Lest	115.7:	But	11.11:	If I
95.22:	Should	115.8:	Who	11.12:	Forget
95.23:	Were	115.9:	And	11.13:	And when
95.24:	Yes,	115.10:	But	11.14:	I answer
95.25:	Deserve	11.1:	Too well *Exalss* [sic]		
95.26:	E're	11.2:	But he		
107.24:	With Looks and Smiles let me regale my Mind	11.3:	Tho'		
		11.4:	If he		
		11.5:	For still		

Ruth Hillary

POEMS

ON

Several Occasions,

Together with a

PASTORAL.

By Mrs. S. F.

LONDON:

Printed, and are to be Sold by *J. Nutt*, near *Stationers-Hall.*

To the Right Honourable

CHARLES

Lord *Halifax*,

Auditor of Her MAJESTIES Exchequer, &c.

My Lord,

WAS not your *Affability* and Condescention, as Conspicuous as your other Graces, I durst not presume on your Protection of these Trifles, some of the first

DEDICATION.

Attempts of my unskilful Muse. Most of the Copies being writ, 'ere I could write Seventeen; long they lay in a neglected Silence, and ne'er design'd to disturb the World; but an unlucky Accident forc'd them to the Press, not giving time for that Examination and Correction, which might have made them, (tho' a smaller) yet more worthy Offering. My Zeal for your Lordship's Name has ever been so Great, I could not persuade my self to pass by this opportunity, of acknowledging it to the World. Which may perhaps too justly Condemn my Lines, but unanimously will applaud my Judgment in the choice of a Patron, as the best of Poets and of Judges. And as such the Representatives of the Mu-

DEDICATION.

Muses Addrest to you, their Obsequies on the late Glory of their Parnassus; a loss my Lord, much o'erpaid by you, whose inimitable Lines, (the soft Diversion of your more leisure Hours) can Charm that World, which was the business of his Life to please; as for those softer Copies which are Interspers'd thro' the whole of mine, I hope your Lordship is of my Opinion, that where the Circumstances do not make Love a Crime, the confessing it can be none. Besides, our Sex is confin'd to so narrow a Sphere of Action, that things of greater Consequence seldom fall within our Notices; so that Love seems the only proper Theme (if any can be so) for a Woman's Pen, especially at the Age they were writ in;

A 3 *and*

DEDICATION.

and some of them were done at the request of Friends, without any other warmth than that of my officious Muse. Excuses and Encomiums are, I think, the common business of Dedications; but I have too many Faults to proceed on the first, and your Lordship too many Excellencies to dare venture on the latter: Your Fame is too Great and Extensive to want or receive Addition from mine, or any the ablest Pens, none but a Genius equal to your own, can do Justice to your Merit. Forgive, my Lord, a silence which proceeds from a profound Veneration of those Noble and Divine Qualifications, which are beyond the Power of Rhetorick, and a Theme so truly Great, that even Eloquence itself
would

DEDICATION.

would want Expression. These Poems (except those on Mr. Dryden,) tho' writ long since, I offer to your Lordship with all their Pristine Bloom, unsully'd by a vulgar touch, not handed round the Town for Opinion and Amendments; but just snatcht from their Recluse in all their native Rudeness and Simplicity, presume for Shelter from your hospitable Hand. They never were abroad before, nor e'er seen but by my own Sex, some of which have favour'd me with their Complements, and I was too much a Woman to refuse them But, my Lord, I detain you from their Ingenious Lines, which I hope will make some Atonement for my Defects, and obtain a Pardon, at least, for the Ambition of Publickly own-

DEDICATION.

owning my value for your Lordship, and for begging your Protection, for your Lordship's

moſt Humble,

and Obedient Servant,

S. F. E.

To

To Mrs. S. F. on her Poems.

OH! say what happy Muse informs thy Lyre,
Or do the sacred Nine, thy Breast inspire;
That thus we see in each judicious Line,
Nature and Art in beauteous Order shine,
The Numbers easy and the Thoughts Divine.
No more let haughty Man with fierce disdain,
Despise the Product of a Female brain,
But read thy Works, there view thy spacious (Mind,
Thy Reason clear, thy Fancy unconfin'd;
And then be just to thy immortal Fame,
And with due Honours celebrate thy Name.
In thy harmonious Strains at once admire,
Orinda's Judgment, and *Astrea*'s Fire.
Many are in Poetick Annals found,
Whose Brows with never fading Laurels bound,
For some one Grace were by *Apollo* Crown'd:

Of

To Mrs. S. F. &c.

Of generous Friendship, this compos'd her Song,
And that with Love still Charm'd the list'ning
(Throng.
Another in Philosophy excells,
And pleasing Wonders tunefully Reveals;
But thou alone on every Theme can'st write,
That task was left for thy superior Wit.

J. H.

To Mrs. S. F. *on her Poems.*

Hail to *Clarinda*, dear *Euterpe* Hail,
 Now we shall Conquer, now indeed pre-
  (vail;
Clarinda will her charming Lines expose,
And in her Strength we vanquish all our Foes.
To these Triumphant Lays, let each repair,
A sacred Sanction to the writing Fair;
Mankind has long upheld the Learned Sway,
And Tyrant Custom forc'd us to obey.
Thought Art and Science did to them belong,
And to assert our selves was deem'd a Wrong,
But we are justify'd by thy immortal Song:
Come ye bright Nymphs a lasting Garland bring,
In never fading Verse, *Clarinda*'s Praises sing;
Read o're her Works, see how Genuine Nature fires,
Observe the sweetness which her Pen inspires.

From

To Mrs. S. F. &c.

From thence grow Wife, from thence your
     (Thoughts improve
Here's Judgment piercing Senfe and softer Love;
To idle Gayeties true Wit prefer,
Strive all ye thinking Fair, to Copy her.

M. P.

To Mrs. S. F. on her incomparable Poems.

THou Champion for our Sex go on and show
    Ambitious Man what Womankind can do
In vain they boast of large Scholastick Rules,
Their skill in Arts and Labour in the Schools.
What various Tongues and Languages acquir'd,
How fam'd for Policy, for Wit admir'd;
Their solid Judgment in Philosophy,
The Metaphysicks, Truths, and Poetry,
Since here they'll find themselves outdon by thee.
Thy matchless Thoughts, and flowing Numbers (sweet,
And lofty Flights, in just Conjunction meet;
Thy mighty Genius can each Subject trace,
The best can equal and to none give Place.
Sappho the Great, whom by report we know,
Would yield her Laurels were she living now,
And strait turn Chast, **to gain a** Friend of you:

To Mrs. S. F. *&c.*

Of you! to whom we all Obedience pay,
And at your Feet our humble Tribute lay,
Whilst all around, your Beams dart like the God
(of Day;
We bask with Pleasure in your Glorious shine,
And read and wonder at your Verse Divine.

S. C.

To my Ingenious Friend Mrs. S. F. on her Poems.

Come ev'ry Muse with Fire and Garlands too,
   Inspire my Breast adorn *Clarinda*'s Brow;
(Cypress and Mirtle with the Laurel twine,
Three Boughs of each, with Heavenly skill com-
                               (bine,
The mystick Number suits the sacred Nine,)
She does the force of every Passion tell,
None ever Lov'd, or Greiv'd, or Prais'd so well.
Sometimes she soars aloft a *Pindar*'s height,
In a bright Track nigh lost to human Sight;
Then gently slides into a softer Strain,
And does with Loves and Graces entertain:
In Panegyricks just to that Degree,
'Tis all complaisant Truth, not nauseous Flattery;
And when her Muse Satyrick would appear,
'Tis without air of Spite, and yet severe.

Then

To Mrs. S. F. &c.

Then in deep Thought reflects on human kind,
And traces Fate thro' her mysterious Wind:
To ev'ry Theme she does her Genius bend,
While every Art and Grace officiously attend.
Such sacred Beauties grace her lays Divine,
Pæan's immortal Beams shine Bright in every Line;
In *Virgil, Ovid, Martial* we prefer,
Some single Gift, but we have all in her.
Forbear by humble Muse, thou art unfit,
To celebrate her various turns of Wit.
Let the soft Pen, who great *Pastora* Mourn'd,
To more delightful rural Strains be turn'd;
And sing *Clarinda*'s Fame, whose tender Lays,
Next to his own, deserve immortal Praise.

E. C.

THE CONTENTS.

	Page.
Friendship	1
The Extacy,	2
To the Honourable Robert Boyle	11
Satyr *against the Muses*	14
To the Queen	17
The Liberty	19
To the Lady Cambell	21
On my leaving London	23
Repulse to Alcander	25
To Mr. Norris *on his Idea of Happiness*	27
The Retreat	31
To one who in Love, set a Figure	33
To Phylaster	34
At my leaving Cambridge	35
Orrabella *Marry'd to an Old Man*	36
To Alexis on his Absence	38
A Song	39
Love	40
Song	ibid.
To one who said I must not Love	42

The CONTENTS.

On the Death of Statyra	44
On ———being tax'd with Simony	46
An occasional Copy to Mr. Joshua Barns	47
A Song on Mrs. S——	48
The Fate	49
A Song	51
On a Gentleman and his Wife visiting, he Sleeping the while	52
The Vision	53
The Power of Love	55
To Mrs. B---g---le	56
The Invocation	58
On the Author of Religion by Reason	60
On Atheism	61
On a Sermon Preach'd on these Words, ye have sold your selves for Nought	64
A Song	64
On my leaving S——y	66
The Gratitude	68
On my Wedding day	70
The Fatality	72
An Ode on the Death of John Dryden Esq;	74
The Advice	80
To Thyrsis, on his Pastoral on Mr. Creech	84
Delia to Phraartes on his Playing Cæsar Borgia	86
To Clarona drawing Alexis Picture, and presenting it to me	88
A Song	90
Erato the Amorous Muse on the Death of John Dryden Esq;	91

Delia

The CONTENTS.

Delia *to* Phraartes, *on his mistake about 3 Ladys*   94
To Marina   97
Euterpe *the Lyrick Muse, on the Death* John Dryden *Esq*;   98
Terpsichore *a Lyrick Muse, on the Death of* John Dryden *Esq*;   104
The Platonick   106
The Emulation   108
To Mr. Yalden, *on his Temple of Fame*   110
On the Death of K. William   111
To Mr. N. Tate *Esq; on the Queen's Picture*   114
To Moneses   117

Errata,

ERRATA.

Page 9. l. 7. *Theys* r. *These*, p. 12. l. 9. *Sublumary* r. *Sublunary*, p. 13. l. 16. r. *Des-Cartes, More*, p. 15. l. 9. *Schreiks* r. *Shrieks* p. 15. l. 10. *Vesevius* r. *Vesuvius*, p. 16. l. 17. *Plague* r. *Plagues*, p. 17. l. 7. *With* r. *In*, p. 32. l. 4. *secure* r. *serene*, l. 5. *poor* r. *more*, p. 33. l. 16. r. *one*, p. 47. l. 9. *Submisely* r. *Submissly*, p. 63. l. 20. *error* r. *errors*, p. 78 l. 19. *fram'd* r. *fam'd*, p. 88. l. 14. *tho'* r. *but*, p. 92. l. 12. *sight* r. *sigh'd*, p. 95. l. 4. r. *are*, p. 106. l. 10. *unweary* r. *unwary*, p. 111. l. 18. *thee* r. *their*, p. 113. l. 4 *Tryton* r. *Trytons*, p. 115. l. 13 *my* r. *thy*.

On Friendship.

Friendship (the great persuit of noble Minds)
Passion in abstract, void of all designs;
Each generous Pen, doth celebrate thy Fame,
And yet I doubt, thou'rt nothing but a Name.
Some pregnant Fancy, in a raptur'd height,
Produc'd this mighty notional Delight.
The Muses virtuosal Chymistry,
To turn all Fortunes to Felicity;
'Tis fancy'd well, and this I dare ingage,
Were all Men Friends, 'twould be the golden Age:
But tell me where, this Extract may be found,
And what Ingredients make the Rich Compound;
Or in what Soul, is that true kindly heat,
That can this great Experiment compleat.
Sometimes a fond good Nature lights upon
A soft and civil Temper like its own;
Strait they resolve to be those happy things,
Which when combin'd, pity contending Kings:

Yet e'er they reach these sublimated Joys,
They'r poorly lost, in Treachery or Toys.
The mighty Notions of the exalted State,
Sink to a vulgar Commerce, or Debate:
Sure, like the Chymick Stone, it was design'd,
But to Imploy the curious searching Mind,
In the persuit of what, none e'er shall find;
Their Quality's I'm sure do prove all one,
Who trusts too much to either, is undone.

The Extacy.

I.

Mount, Mount, my Soul on high,
  Cut through the spacious Sky;
Scale the great Mountainous heaps that be,
Betwixt the upper World, and thee.
Stop not, till thou the utmost Region know,
Leave all the shining Worlds below:
  Then take thy Noble flight,
Into the sacred Magazine of Light,
View the bright, the Etherial Throne
Of the great, the Almighty ONE.

The Extacy.

All the Miriades of shining Hosts survey,
With the seraphick blazing throng;
Celebrating their Eternal Day,
   With an Eternal Song.
In vain my dazled Soul would gaze around,
(The beatifick Glorys so confound)
It must be quite disrob'd, e'er tread this Holy
                           (Ground.

II.

   Descend thou daring Spirit, think 'tis fair,
If thou may'st traverse the inferior Air;
Content with humbler Curiosities,
   View the expanded Skies,
With radient Worlds, 'tis richly deck'd,
By the Almighty Architect.
   Mount *Charles*'s Wain,
Drive over all the Etherial Plain,
   And to augment thy Speed,
With blazing Comets lash the Restive Steeds.
Make them neigh aloud and foam,
Till all the Sky a milky way become;
   What tho' they Fret and Rage,
   To pass their wonted Stage.

The Extacy.

Make them praunce o'er all the amazing Place,
   Quite to the empty Space,
And as ye go, see what Inhabitants there are,
   In every World, of every Star;
Their Shape, their Manners and their State,
   Write in Journal as ye go,
And to the inquireing Earth relate;
   By droping it below.
When weary'd with your universal round,
Let the Sphears harmonious sound,
Refresh and Charm your Spirits, till they be
Fit to fly back to their first ventur'd one Immensity.
But oh! the Harmonys too soft, too sweet,
The Eternal strains too ravishingly great,
I cannot bear such Transports yet,
Well then, I'll have these mighty heights and go
And over-look the little Globe below.

III.

In this small Plat, is vast variety,
   To entertain my Curiosity:
Here the great Waters of the mighty deep,
'Their fixt amazing bounds do keep;

The Extacy.

In vain they Rage and Roar,
But dare not touch on the restraining Shoar.
Here finny Herds of th' smallest sort,
   Safely Play and Sport;
Wanton I'th' deep, with no more Danger then
   The pastimes of Leviathan.
   Here does in Triumph ride,
The stately Trophies of *Britania*'s Pride:
Her Ships which to the *Indies* Trade,
   Such Noble Fabricks are made;
   And so numerous appear,
The frighted Natives do our Traffick fear,
   And doubt we will invade.
   Securely too in these,
   They visit the Antipodes.
From *Brittain* they, the courteous Race begun,
A piece of complaisance unknown,
To all but civil Drake and the obliging Sun.
Neptune with pompous Pride does bear
Those glorious Terrors, Ships of War.
The floating Tow'rs they in *Battalia* draw;
   Keep all the circling Reals in awe.
Yet these vast Bodies, the soft Waters bear:
So the great Bird of *Jove*, mounts in the trackless
                                 (Air.

On the smooth Floods, the swelling Billows rise,
As if the liquid Mountains touch'd the Skies :
Then quick they plunged, with an Impetuous hast,
And seem'd to speak Destruction as they pass'd,
Yet Arm'd with Avarice and Curiosities,
Men scorn the Dangers, of the threatning Seas.

IV.

Next on the solid Parts, I cast my Eye,
   Did vast scorcht Desert spie ;
Which untamed Beasts, and Monsters bred,
   By them alone inhabited.
I saw huge Mountains of uncommon Earth,
   Some beleh with Terror forth ;
    A sulpherous Smoak,
Loud as amazing Thunder spoke,
From the unexhausted Bowel came,
Ashes and Stones, evacuated by Flame ;
Remote from these are frigid Mountains too,
   Thick cloth'd in fleecy Snow.
Some by restringent Air congeal'd as hard,
As if with Adamintine barr'd :

Stupen-

The Extacy.

Stupendious Rocks of hideous Stones I found,
Whose dangerous Heads, lean'd on the threaten'd
(Ground.
Deep in Earths center, far from human sight,
I search'd with intellectual Light ;
   (Pierc'd to the gloomy Ray,
Where subterenean Fires, in silence play,
Like the faint Glimps of an imprison'd Day.)
Where unmolested Streams with gentle force,
Press, to their Primeveal source ;
(And sometimes upward, gush thro' poreous Earth,
Give to the healing Baths, a useful Birth ;)
In its more wealthy parts, the Minerals lay,
And ponderous Mettals shining Nerves display:
In her bright Bowels, radiant Gems remains,
Till cruel Man defects, and rends her Saphir vains.
   With Grief and Wonder I behold,
    The Noble, but mischevious Gold ;
(Oh! with what Toyl, and mighty Pain,
Men the inchanting Mettle gain.
This Tyrant Clay Lords it o'er human kind,
Tho' they themselves in dirt, at first the Monarch
(find;

The Extacy.

Lets their Stupidity, no more upbraid,
Who worshipp'd Gods, which their own Hands
(had made,
Since we're by Gold to greater Crimes betray'd.
Our Country, Faith, Friends, Honour for its fold,
Nay, Heaven and Love, is sacrific'd to Gold;
We're worse Idolaters, then they,
Who only Homage, gave since we mischeviously
(obey.

V.

Then the habitable World appear'd,
By Art, vast Towns and pompous Temples rear'd.
The pleasing Fields, awhile detain'd my sight,
  With a severe delight:
The flowry Meads, with various Colours dy'd,
And smiling Nature, in her verdant Pride;
Here ancient Woods, and blooming Groves,
  (Fit recesses, for celestial Loves,)
Where purling Streams, glide with delightful hast,
On whose cool Banks, are spreading Willows
(plac'd:
The weary'd Birds Sings on the shading Bough,
In such glad Notes, as Nature did bestow.

The

The Extacy.

The bleating Flocks and Herds, o'erspread the
(Plains,
And recompence the joyful Peasants pains.
   Here the unenvy'd Village stood,
Rais'd of native Clay, and neighbouring Wood.
The Inhabitants as void of Pride, or Art,
Blest with plain Diet, and an honest Heart;
Theys Plow'd the Ground, and Sow'd the pregnant
(Grain,
Reap'd joyfully; the plentious Crop again:
Innocent Slaves, to whose rude Care we owe,
The chief supports of Life, and utmost needs be-
(low.

Remoter helps are Springs to Luxury,
Rich Wines and Spices, and the Tyrian die,
Do not our Wants, but Wantonness supply.
Here in his humble Cott, the Rustick lies,
Knows not the Curse, of being Great or Wise;
Ambition, Treachery, and Fear,
   Are Strangers here.
Secure and quiet they go plodding on,
Happy, because too mean to be undone.

                       Then

VI.

Then I espy'd from far,
Troops of shining Men, ingag'd in War,
Their artful Weapons, are with Rage imploy'd,
And Man, by Man, is Savagely destroy'd:
   Poor mercenary Slaves they die,
   But seldom know for why;
Oh! what Confusions here I cannot bear,
These horrid Groans that reach my distant Ear
From slaugher'd heaps, of dying Accents there.
Sometimes wast Towns in Flames appear,
Huge Castles mount, and shatter in the Air,
   But ah! what pity 'tis,
Mankind should Glory in such Arts as these;
Then to the populous Cities, I repair'd,
   Found they were little less insnar'd;
Tho' not Alarm'd with mighty noise of Wars,
Yet curs'd with grating, private Jars,
Envy and Strife, Self-Interest, and Deceits,
Extravagance and Noise, her Fate compleats.
Then I survey'd the splendid Court,
Found pageant Follies, Revelling and Sport,

Base Falshood, Lust, Ambition, Emnity,
  Soft wanton Intervals, and Luxury,
Destructive Flattery, and hateful Pride,
  And all the City Sins beside.
  Thinks I, what shall I do,
  If I must live again below,
For I remember'd that I had been there,
  And a return to Earth, did fear.
Grant ye bless'd Powers, said I,
If I must downwards fly;
I may Descend upon the blooming Plain,
Bless'd with the harmless Nymph, and humble
                                    (Swain,
There let me ever undisturb'd remain.

On the Honourable Robert Boyl's, Notion of Nature.

'TIS bravely done, great *Boyle* has disen-
                                    (thron'd,
The Goddess Nature, so unjustly Crown'd,
And by the Learn'd so many Ages own'd.

Refuge of Atheists, whose supine desire,
Pleas'd with that Stage, no farther will aspire:
It damps the Theists too, while they assign,
To Nature, what's done by a Power divine.
We know not how, nor where, to ascribe events,
While she's thus Rival to Omnipotence;
Sure that alone, the mighty Work can do,
The Power that did create, can Govern too:
It is not like our sublumary Kings,
That must be circumscrib'd to place, and things,
Whose straighten'd Power, doth Ministers Elect,
That must for them remoter business act,
The Omnipresence, of the Power Divine,
Argues it need no Deputies assign;
Nor is't beneath the Glory of his State,
To Rule, Protect the Beings he create:
But stop my Pen, blush at thy weak pretence,
Tis *Boyle*, not thee, that must the World con-
(vince;
Boyle the great Champion of Providence.
Whose conquering Truths in an Inquiry drest,
Have celebrated Nature dispossest;
Not the Vice gerent of Heavens settled Rules,
But nice Idea of the erring Schools.

Fate,

On the Honourable R. Boyl's,

Fate, Fortune, Chance, all notional and vain,
The floating Fictions of the Poet's brain;
The World rejects, yet stupidly prefers,
This wild Chimera of Philosophers:

This more insinuating Notion lay,
Unquestion'd till you made your brave Assay,
Which doth the daring Sceptick more confute,
Than a suspected Orthodox dispute.
They can't pretend Int'rest, thy Lines doth Bribe
With which they censure, the Canonick Tribe:
'Twas Love of Truth alone, thy Pen did move,
Nor none but thee, could so successful prove.
Methinks I all the School-mens Shades espy,
Tending thy Tryumphs of Philosophy,
And all the pregnant Naturist of Yore,
From the Great Stagarite, to descartes and more;
Resigning their Gigantick Notions now,
And only what you write for Truth allow.
See they have all their renounc'd Volumes brought,
(Bidding Mankind believe, what you have Taught;)
Asham'd they've been, renown'd so many Years,
Each from his blushing Brow his Laurel tares:

With

Satyr, *against the Muses.*

With their own Hands, in one just Wreath they (twine,
Adorning that victorious Head of thine.
And shall my Female Pen, thy Praise pretend,
When Angels only, can enough commend,
In Songs, which like themselves, can know no (End.

Satyr *against the Muses.*

BY my abandon'd Muse, I'm not inspir'd,
Provok'd by Malice, and with Rage I'm fir'd.
Fly, fly, my Muse from my distracted Breast,
Who e'er has thee, must be with Plagues possest:
Fool that I was, e'er to sollicite you,
Who make not only Poor, but wretched too.
Happy I liv'd, for almost Eight years time,
Curss'd be your Skill, you taught me then to (Rhime:
The Jingling noise, shed its dark Influence,
On my then pleased, unwary Innocence,
I scarce have had one happy Moment since.

Here

Here all the Spite and Rage of Womankind,
Cannot enough advance my threatning Mind,
Let Furies too, be in the Consort join'd.
Passion, that common Rage, I here refuse,
Call Hell itself, to curse my Torturing Muse;
Not the calm Author of blest Poetry,
But the black Succubus of Misery:
There let her sit, with her Infernal Chyme,
And put the Schreiks and Groans of Fiends in
(Rhime.
May their *Parnassus*, like *Vesevius* burn,
Their Laurels wither, or to Cypriss turn;
May Stuff like *Hopkin*'s Rhyme, degrade their
(Fame,
And none but Ballad-makers use their Name:
May they despis'd, sad and neglected sit,
Be never thought upon by Men of Wit.
May all the Ills a fond Imperious Dame,
Wishes the Man that dare reject her Flame,
Light upon him, that does commit the Crime,
Of writing any thing, in jingling Rhime;
Nothing like that, to Dangers can expose,
May none be Happy, but what write in Prose.
Curse on the Whimsical, Romanick Fool,
That yielded first, to his Phantastick Rule;

That

That Wit like Morris-dancers must advance,
With Bells at Feet, and in nice measures Dance.
Let pregnant Heads, but think of Poetry,
And just before the Brain-delivery;
Fancy shall make a Prodigy of Wit,
Which soon, as born, shall run upon its Feet:
Sure, 'tis some Necromantick Ordinance,
That Sence, beyond the Circle mayn't advance;
Was all the learned Ancients Courage dead,
That Wit, in Fetters, is tame Captive led?
Had Some oppos'd, when Rhyme at first grew
(bold,
Then her Defeat, not Triumphs had been told?
But now the Plague is grown so populous,
'Tis hard to stop the universal Curse.
Doubtless, they are mistaken who have told
Spightful *Pandora*'s pregnant Box did hold
Plurality of Plague, She only hurl'd
Out Verse alone, and that has damn'd the World.
Curses, in vain, on Poets I bestow;
I'm sure, the greatest is, that they are so;
Fate, send worse if thou can'st, but Rescue me
From trifling torturing wretched Poetry.

To the Queen.

MY trembling Muse, with awful Duty press,
Mong'ſt kneeling crouds, with thy un-
(feign'd Addreſs;
Since meaneſt Slaves, to Altars may repair,
With ſacred Rites, of Sacrifice and Prayer.
Heaven takes the Incenſe, if it is ſincere,
Freely as if the Great, had offer'd there,
Bleſs'd with ſuch hopes, my Muſe, with Proſtrate
(Zeal,
Dare at the Feet of her great Sovereign kneel;
You I revere, like Heaven, not cauſe you'r high,
Not for your Glory; but Divinity.
The radiant Gems, that deck *Britannia*'s Crown,
Ne'er ſhone ſo Bright, till you had put it on;
You, who have condeſcended to a Throne.
In you kind Heaven, the unuſual Bleſſing brings,
Greatneſs and Goodneſs, are conſiſtent Things:
Your Subjects modeſt Merits your regard,
Virtue, not Impudence, now finds Reward;
Goodneſs like yours ſo aws the Bolder ſort,
As makes a Sanctuary of your Court.

To the Queen.

All your Retinue, so reform'd appear,
As if the Golden Age, were Blooming here;
Fix'd like the Sun, superior you dispence,
On all the under World, your blisful Influence.
The Graces in your smiles, with Grandeur move,
And form an Air of Majesty and Love:
Heaven be propitious to my Monarch's Arms,
And make them as Victorious, as her Charms,
Revenge on your proud Foes, their *Salick* Law,
With your fair Hand, their boasted Greatness awe.
Why are we barr'd, or why I Woman made,
Whose Sex forbids to Fight, and to Invade,
Or give my Queen, more than my wish for Aid?
I shall not tremble, at the Launce, or Sword,
Will strait turn *Amazon*, but speak the Word;
Scarce can I curb, my eager loyal Soul,
For you I'd fight, Mankind from Pole to Pole,
Till all the Kingdoms, in one Empire meet,
Then lay the Crown at your Imperial Feet.
They'd bless the Arms, which did their Realms sub-
(due,
And hug the Chains, which made them Slaves to
(you;
May you in Peace, long Rule your Native Land,
And the just Terror, of Ambition stand:

May

May every Subject you protect; Profess
As much as I, and dare to act no less.

The Liberty.

SHall I be one, of those obsequious Fools,
    That square there lives, by Customs scanty
                                (Rules;
Condemn'd for ever, to the puny Curse,
Of Precepts taught, at Boarding-school, or Nurse,
That all the business of my Life must be,
Foolish, dull Trifling, Formality.
Confin'd to a strict Magick complaisance,
And round a Circle, of nice visits Dance,
Nor for my Life beyond the Chalk advance:
The Devil Censure, stands to guard the same,
One step awry, he tears my ventrous Fame.
So when my Friends, in a facetious Vein,
With Mirth and Wit, a while can entertain;
Tho' ne'er so pleasant, yet I must not stay,
If a commanding Clock, bids me away:
But with a sudden start, as in a Fright,
I must be gone indeed, 'tis after Eight.

The Liberty.

Sure these restraints, with such regret we bear,
That dreaded Censure, can't be more severe,
Which has no Terror, if we did not fear;
But let the Bug-bear, timerous Infants fright,
I'll not be scar'd, from Innocent delight :
Whatever is not vicious, I dare do,
I'll never to the Idol Custom bow,
Unless it suits with my own Humour too.
Some boast their Fetters, of Formality,
Fancy they ornamental Bracelets be,
I'm sure their Gyves, and Manacles to me.
To their dull fulsome Rules, I'd not be ty'd,
For all the Flattery that exalts their Pride :
My Sexs forbids, I should my Silence break,
I lose my Jest, cause Women must not speak.
Mysteries must not be, with my search Prophan'd,
My Closet not with Books, but Sweat-meats
(cram'd
A little *China*, to advance the Show,
My *Prayer Book*, and seven *Champions*, or so.
My Pen if ever us'd imploy'd must be,
In lofty Themes of useful Houswifery,
Transcribing old Receipts of Cookery :

And

And what is necessary 'mongst the rest,
Good Cures for Agues, and a cancer'd Breast,
But I can't here, write my *Probatum est.*
My daring Pen, will bolder Sallies make,
And like my self, an uncheck'd freedom take;
Not chain'd to the nice Order of my Sex,
And with restraints my wishing Soul perplex:
I'll blush at Sin, and not what some call Shame,
Secure my Virtue, slight precarious Fame.
This Courage speaks me, Brave, 'tis surely worse,
To keep those Rules, which privately we Curse:
And I'll appeal, to all the formal Saints,
With what reluctance they indure restraints.

To the Lady Cambell, *with a Female Advocate.*

GO, fatal Book, yet happy at the last,
 Since in so fair, so kind a Hand thou'rt
  (plac'd,
(That such a Trifle, e'er should be so grac'd.)
But your Desires, which are to me Commands,
Can charm what e'er you please out of my Hands;

I rather than neglect obliging you,
Expose my Follies, to your nice view:
But hope your Goodness, will one Smile bestow,
On what my tender Infant Muse did do.
Scarce fourteen Years, when I the piece begun,
And in less time than fourteen days 'twas done;
Without design of Publication writ,
And Innocence supply'd, the want of Wit.
But ah! my Poetry, did fatal prove,
And robb'd me of a tender Father's Love;
(I thought that only Men, who writ for Fame,
Or sung lewd Stories, of unlawful Flame,
Were punish'd for, their proud or wanton Crime.
But Children too, must suffer if they'll Rhyme:)
The Present is but mean, which you receive,
Yet cost me more, than all the World can give,
That which I would, with Life itself retrieve.
But Madam, if your Goodness condescend,
And one kind Minute, on this trifle spend;
It will compleat my Happiness at last,
And recompence for all my Sorrows past.

On my leaving London, June *the* 29.

WHat cross impetuous Planets govern me,
    That I'm thus hurry'd on to Misery;
I thought I had been bless'd, a while ago,
But one quick push, plung'd me all o'er in Woe.
My cruel Fate, doth act the Tyrant's part,
And doth Torment me, with a lingering smart;
To make me sensible of greater Pain,
Lets me take Breath, then screws the Rack again;
Ah! where's the Joy, of such precarious Bliss,
That for one smiling short Parenthesis;
I must such tedious horrid Pangs indure,
And neither State, will either kill or cure.
With all Submission, I my Fate implore,
Destroy me quite, or else Torment no more;
At least let not one glimps of Joy appear,
It only makes my Sufferings more severe.
No, here I'll Rule, not sue to you for this,
You cannot tantalize me now with Bliss;
For when you took, my Father's love away,
Perverse as you, I'd not let others stay:
I was not so insensibly undone,
  To hoord up Counters, when my Gold was gone.

Plunder'd of all, I now forsake the Place,
Where all my Joys, and all my Treasure was,
Ah do not now, my wandering Footsteeps
(Trace;
I left the Town, and all Divertisement,
And in a lonely Village am content.
Nor do I ask to be remov'd from hence,
Tho' Man and Beast, are both of equal Sense:
I had not fled, but strongly forc'd by you,
In hast bid Mother, Sisters sad adieu.
I saw them last of all I knew in Town,
Yet all alike to me are Strangers grown;
I almost have forgot I e'er was there,
And the sad Accidents that brought me here.
Ah Fate! pursue me not in this Retreat,
Let me be quiet in this humble Seat:
Let not my Friends know where to send to me,
Lest I grow pleas'd with their Civility.
I'd fain live unconcern'd, not pleas'd nor cross'd,
And be to all the busy World as lost.

The Repulse to Alcander.

WHAT is't you mean, that I am thus ap-
(proach'd,
Dare you to hope, that I may be debauch'd?
For your seducing Words the same implies,
In begging Pity with a soft Surprize,
For one who loves, and sighs, and almost dies.
In ev'ry Word and Action doth appear,
Something I hate and blush to see or hear;
At first your Love for vast Respect was told,
Till your excess of Manners grew too bold,
And did your base, designing Thoughts unfold.
When a Salute did seem to Custom due,
With too much Ardour you'd my Lips pursue;
My Hand, with which you play'd, you'd Kiss
(and Press,
Nay ev'ry Look had something of Address.
Ye Gods! I cry'd, sure he designs to woo,
For thus did amorous *Phylaster* do.
The Youth whose Passion none could disapprove,
When *Hymen* waited to compleat his Love;
But now, when sacred Laws and Vows confine
Me to another what can you design?

At

The Repulse to Alcander.

At firſt, I could not ſee the lewd Abuſe,
But fram'd a thouſand Things for your Excuſe.
I knew that *Bacchus* ſometimes did inſpire
A ſudden Tranſport, tho' not laſting Fire;
For he no leſs than *Cupid* can make kind,
And force a Fondneſs which was ne'er deſign'd
Or thought you'd travel'd far, and it might chance,
To be the foreign Mode of Complaiſance.
Till you ſo oft your amorous Crimes repeat,
That to permit you would make mine as great;
Nor ſtopt you here but languiſhingly ſpake,
That Love which I endeavour'd to miſtake:
What ſaw you in me, that could make you vain,
Or any thing expect, but juſt Diſdain?
I muſt confeſs I am not quite ſo Nice,
To Damn all little Gallantries for Vice;
(But I ſee now my Charity's miſplac'd,
If none but ſullen Saints can be thought Chaſt:)
Yet know, Baſe Man, I ſcorn your lewd Amours,
Hate them from all, not only cauſe they're yours.
Oh ſacred Love! let not the World prophane,
Thy Tranſports, thus to Sport, and Entertain;
The Beau, with ſome ſmall Artifice of's own,
Can make a Treat, for all the wanton Town:

To Mr. Norris,

I thought my self secure, within these Shades,
But your rude Love, my Privacy invades,
Affronts my Virtue, hazards my just Fame,
Why should I suffer, for your lawless Flame?
For oft 'tis known, through Vanity and Pride,
Men boast those Favours which they are deny'd:
Or others Malice, which can soon discern;
Perhaps may see in you some kind Concern.
So scatter false Suggestions of their own,
That I love too: Oh! Stain to my Renown;
No, I'le be Wise, avoid your Sight in time,
And shun at once the Censure and the Crime.

To Mr. Norris, *on his Idea of Happiness.*

I.

IF Pythagorick notions would agree,
  With sublimated Christianity;
What mighty Soul, shall I allow,
  Informs thy Body now;
   For when did such appear,
Sure the belov'd Disciple's Soul is here.

Not

Not us'd since then, but kept above,
And taught a more extatick Love;
The Understanding more inlarg'd and free,
    Each generous Faculty
Refin'd, Improv'd, made more compleat,
    In the seraphick Seat.
The brightest warmest of th' exalted Quire,
Flaming with Rays of beatifick Fire;
Such seems thy elevated Soul to be,
And not the usual sort gave to Mortality.

II.

The great, the Eternal God of Love,
Took Pity on us from above;
    He could no longer see,
Our Souls wrapt in Obscurity:
But sent thee like, a bright celestial Ray,
To clear our Sight, and to direct the Way;
    To the Etherial Courts of Bliss,
The only great, and lasting Happiness,
The active native Principle of Love,
    We found did move
    By an internal Influence,
But 'twas toward some object of the Sense:

Effects and Causes were not underſtood,
We only knew we wiſht for Good,
And would with Joy each glimpſe purſue,
Reſolve to faſten there, and think 'twas true.
In vain we thought our Love was fixt,
    For all thoſe Joys were intermixt
With Diſappointments and Deceit,
Our ſtrugling Souls themſelves did cheat:
Still they deſir'd and lov'd, but were not bleſt,
    Nor found they Reſt,
Till thy bright Pen markt out the happy Prize,
Taught us at once to love and to be wiſe.

III.

Thou doſt diſect our weak diſtemper'd Soul,
Diſcover'ſt the Diſeaſe and mak'ſt us whole;
Preſcrib'ſt ſuch Methods, which if we obey,
We ſhall no longer doat on Clay,
Which long our vitiated Souls have fed,
But ſhall have Appetite to Celeſtial Bread.
    We ſhall no longer fondly play,
        With Trifles on the way,
But climb the Hill with a delightful haſt,
And feaſt our Souls at thy divine Repaſt.

But

But left, like doubtful or unthankful Guest,
We should neglect the Royal Feast;
Thou, to incourage our appearance there,
Hast kindly given us a Bill of Fare.

IV.

By powerful Energy of Thoughts divine,
Thou didst thy Soul raise and refine,
With strong Impulse it did upward move,
Mounting on eager Wings of Love;
Through all th' inferior Courts it made its way,
To the bright Spring of everlasting day;
   Did all the amazing Glories see,
   And what it shou'd hereafter be,
Saluted by the soft Seraphick Quire,
Who's Anthems all its Faculties inspire,
But flasht to mighty Rays of sacred Fire.
For the refulgent Glories were too great,
It could not bear such Raptures, yet,
Till Immortality had made it more compleat:
It could no longer stay, no longer view,
   Then down again it flew,
Did with Angelick Radiance shine,
   Inspir'd with Sapience divine.

The Retreat.

It doth its bright Etherial Voyage tell,
And in what Bliss departed Souls do dwell:
All this in pure and pregnant Elegance we hear,
Plain as Corporeal Organs can declare,
That when we read thy Lines we almost think
(we're there.

The Retreat.

ADieu to all the splendid Gallantry,
Complaisant Pleasures, modish Gaiety;
Airy Delights, imaginary Joys,
Fashions, Entertainments, Wit and Noise;
To all the Follies of my former State,
All that's Genteel, or Popular, or Great.
I'll move no longer in this gaudy Sphear,
I've been gaz'd at enough, 'tis time to disappear.
Without Concern, I'll leave the glittering Seat;
No, not the softest Sigh shall sound retreat,
Left Fate should over-hear, mistrust my Flight,
Pursue me now, and so undo me quite.
In these soft Shades, I no Misfortune fear,
For she will never think to find me here;

My Joys, shall be by her no more betray'd,
I'll cheat her now, in this kind Masquerade;
While she in Noise and Crowds doth search for
(me
I'll lie Secure in safe Obscurity.
A silent Village doth poor Pleasures yield,
Or harmless Sports of the delightful Field;
Then all the pageant Glories of a Throne,
Luxurious Pleasures of the wanton Town.
Here is the Copy of lost Paradice,
The pure and spotless Quintessence of Bliss:
All the safe Pastimes Mankind can enjoy,
Which Innocence delight, but not destroy:
Here I am blest in these secure Abodes,
As once in Shades were the retiring Gods:
These silvan Joys know no surprizing Strife,
This is to live, whilst others spend a Life:
Here is the *Summum Bonum* of the Earth,
Here the renowned Poets had their Birth;
Or hither, from the noisy World retir'd,
Here their great Souls, with noble Raptures fir'd.
Philosophers of old, in Solitude,
Their own resisting Passions first subdu'd;
Then with good Precepts civiliz'd the Rude:

They

To who in Love, set a Figure.

They knew a Court or City would molest
The calm Conceptions of a studious Breast.
Here the *Mautuan* Swain gain'd all his Bays
To Solitude his unmatch'd Pen doth raise,
Disserved Trophies of immortal Praise.
How many Monarchs weary of their State,
Have quit their Glories for a mean retreat;
Thought silent Shades far happier than Thrones,
That Garlands sat much easier than Crowns.
Then why's the wond'ring World amaz'd at me,
For leaving Fraud and Infidelity?
The poor mistaken World who places Joys
In splendid Popularity and Noise,
When after all it's Search it must conclude,
'Tis in a Friend, and well-chose Solitude.

To who in Love, set a Figure.

IN vain alas ye search your artless Books,
   A lover's Fates writ in his Mistris's Looks;
'Tis to no purpose that ye gaze ith' Skys,
There are no Stars like her propitious Eyes.
When Hearts are lost to set a Figure vain,
None but the Thief knows if you'll hav't again.

To Philaster.

Your *Venus* ask, not *Mercury*'s Aid intreat,
For he knows nothing of an amorous Cheat:
'Tis she alone that can the Mystery tell,
Read but her Looks they are infallible;
Consult the upper World for Death and Wars,
She is Love's Heaven, her Eyes the only Stars:
Since her kind Influence hath attracted you,
She may admit of a Conjunction too.

To Philaster.

GO perjur'd Youth and court what Nymph you please,
Your Passion now is but a dull Disease,
With worn-out Sighs deceive some list'ning Ear,
Who longs to know how 'tis and what Men swear,
She'l think they'r new from you; 'cause so to her.
Poor cousin'd Fool, she ne'er can know the Charms
Of being first encircled in thy Arms.
When all Love's Joys were innocent and gay,
As fresh and blooming as the new-born day.
Your Charms did then with native Sweetness flow,
The forc'd-kind Complaisance you now bestow,
Is but a false agreeable Design,
But you had Innocence when you were mine,
And all your Words, and Smiles, and Looks divine.

How

At my leaving Cambridge, &c.

How Proud, methinks, thy Miſtriſs does appear
In ſully'd Cloths, which I'd no longer wear;
Her Boſom too with wither'd Flowers dreſt,
Which loſt their Sweets in my firſt choſen Breaſt;
Perjur'd impoſing Youth, cheat who you will,
Supply defect of Truth with amorous Skill;
Yet thy Addreſs muſt needs inſipid be,
Fot the firſt Ardour of thy Soul was all poſſeſs'd
(by me

At my leaving Cambridge Auguſt *the* 14*th,* Extempore.

CAmbridge adieu! I ne'er ſhall ſee thee more,
Nor feaſt my Soul at Learning's mighty Store;
Not one freſh Drop of thy ambroſial Senſe,
To quench my Thirſt at learned *Cham*'s Expence;
Apollo's Fountain I muſt ever quit,
Who's only *Nectar* is the ſtreams of Wit;
I thy fair Colleges no more ſhall ſee,
Each *Greece, Rome, Athens,* in Epitomy;
The antient infant Learning which they taught,
Could only here be to Perfection brought;

· They've

They've finish'd all, each long hid Spring discern,
The Gods themselves may hover here and learn;
And if in every Grace they would advance,
Let *B*—give Wit, and *G*—teach Complaisance;
To th' sacred *Vatican* no more I come,
But grieve like *Ovid* when excluded *Rome*.

To Orabella, *Marry'd to an old Man.*

TEll me fair Nymph who justly had design'd,
   A charming Youth to suit your equal Mind;
What did seduce you thus to match with one,
Whom if by Nature made she'll scarcely own?
For form'd so many Centuries ago,
She has forgot if he's her Work or no;
I think the way to do his Reverence right,
Is to suppose him a Pre-Adamite:
Your blooming Youth his Age beyond decay,
Will teach censorious Malice what to say,
Who spite of Virtue will your Fame betray.
What strong Persuasions made you thus to wed,
With such a Carcass scandalize your Bed?
Sure 'twas no earthly Gain that charm'd you to't,
Nothing but hopes of Heaven should make me do't:

But

To an old Man.

But since there's other ways to gain that Bliss,
Dispatching Martyrdom I wou'd not miss,
To be secur'd, could I but 'scape from this.
The monster Twin whose Brother grew from's Side,
With all the stench he suffer'd when he dy'd,
Is a just Emblem of so yok'd a Bride.
But Ptisick, Gout and Palsie have their Charms,
And did intice you to his trembling Arms:
Kind amorous Glances from his hollow Eyes,
Did your gay Breast with rapturous Joys surprize
Ah! who can blame to see a yielding Maid,
By all these blooming Charms to Love betray'd.
Oh! for a vestal's Coldness to resist
The tempting Softness in such Beauties drest.
The bright Idea soon dissolves in Air,
And in it's room the Picture of Despair.
A moving Skeleton he seems to be,
Nature's antientest Anatomy.
Worth Observation, hang him up therefore
In *Gresham* College, and I'll ask no more.

To Alexis, *on his absence.*

SAY, lovely Youth, why all this niceneſs ſhown,
   Is modeſt Paſſion, ſo offenſive grown?
I'll not oblige too far, nor force my Charms,
To tempt your Coyneſs to my ſlighted Arms:
Give me but leave, with ſecret ſighs to Gaze,
And ſilent Joys, view that dear fatal Face.
I never dreſs'd, nor ſmil'd, us'd no ſoft Art,
No little Amorous cheat to win your Heart,
Nor knew in mine you had ſo great a Part;
Till from my Sight you cautiouſly remov'd,
Then, not till then, I knew how well I lov'd:
'Twas my Advice, you ſhould awhile abſent,
I ne'er deſign'd it for a Baniſhment.
But wiſely you, as if you fear'd your Fate,
Shun what you would not Love, and cannot hate;
Yet ſpite of all your Vanity and Care,
Know my *Alexis*, that I have you here:
Here in my Breaſt, your deareſt Image glows,
Warms every Wiſh, and ſoftens all my Vows.
Inſpires my Muſe, to wanton in your Charms,
And feaſt on Joys, which are deny'd my Arms:

A Song.

In melting strains, she shall my Passion tell,
Describe those lovely Eyes, and Smiles so well;
Till every Nymph who my soft Lines shall see,
Sighs and Adores, and owns she loves like me.
That Shape, that Mein, that dear undoing Tongue,
With thousand unknown Charms shall fill my
(Song,
To glad the listening World and make it last as
(long.
With an Eternal blast the trump of Fame,
Will sound *Alexis* and *Clarinda*'s Name,
Your matchless Graces, my unequall'd Flame.
You shall this fondness of my Muse forgive,
And tho' not in my Arms, in my soft numbers live:
While warlike Heroes who are half Divine, (thine.
Shall have their Glories sung, in meaner Lays than

A SONG.

Curse on this Virtue Constancy,
  Of which we're vainly Proud;
It like a Crime doth Torture me,
Since all my softer thoughts of Bliss,
And ev'ry kind and tender Wish,
Is on a careless thankless Swain bestow'd.

I with more ease could bear my Fate,
Forgive his Cruelty,
If stupidly our Sex he hate:
But he doth Smile on every Fair,
The partial Curse I cannot bear,
For, oh he's kind! he's kind! to all but me.

Love.

LOVE, like Original Sin, in all does dwell,
Fools sighs in private, and the Witty tell;
Boast they'r fond Passions in repeated Rhymes,
That other Reigning Mischief of the Times:
The Learn'd asham'd to own their Amorous Pain,
Vent the warm Raptures in a Pious strain,
Sigh, Languish, Die, (tho' for a Mortal fair,)
In Lays Divine, like *Quarles* and *Arwaker*.

A SONG.

PHylaster's grown unkind,
The lovely perjur'd Youth,
Tho' by sacred Oaths confind;
Has now lost all his Truth.

A Song.

He swore ten thousand times,
By all the Powers above,
Wish'd they would revenge his Crimes,
If he was false to Love.

Yet, spite of all he's gone,
Fled my once dear Imbrace ;
And now I must be undone,
For some new Shape or Face.
Ye heedless Nymphs beware,
How you receive my Swain,
Ah ! believe not tho' he Swear,
For he will change again.

The sullen part of Love,
Doth only Torture us,
When the Men please to remove,
They make some new Address.
With Passion like soft Truths,
They court fresh gentle scorn ;
We must wait till other Youths,
Do want to be forsworn.

To One who said I must not Love.

Bid the fond Mother spill her Infants Blood,
The hungry Epicure not think of Food;
Bid the *Antartick* touch the *Artick* Pole:
When these obey I'll force Love from my Soul.
As Light and Heat compose the Genial Sun,
So Love and I essentially are one:
E'er your Advice a thousand ways I try'd
To ease the inherent Pain, but 'twas deny'd;
Tho' I resolv'd, and griev'd, and almost dy'd.
Then I would needs dilate the mighty Flame,
Play the Coquet, hazard my dearest Fame:
The modish Remedy I try'd in vain,
One thought of him contracts it all again.
Weary'd at last, curst *Hymen*'s Aid I chose;
But find the fetter'd Soul has no Repose.
Now I'm a double Slave to Love and Vows:
As if my former Sufferings were too small,
I've made the guiltless Torture-Criminal.
E'er this I gave a loose to fond Desire,
Durst smile, be kind, look, languish and admire,
With wishing Sighs fan the transporting Fire.

But

To One who said I must not Love. 43

But now these soft Allays are so like Sin,
I'm forc'd to keep the mighty Anguish in;
Check my too tender Thoughts and rising Sighs,
As well as eager Arms and longing Eyes.
My Kindness to his Picture I refrain,
Nor now imbrace the lifeless lovely Swain.
To press the charming Shade tho' thro' a Glass,
Seems a Platonick breach of *Hymen*'s Laws,
Thus nicely fond, I only stand and gaze.
View the dear conq'ring Form that forc'd my Fate,
Till I become as motionless as that.
My sinking Limbs deny their wonted Aid,
Fainting I lean against my frighted Maid;
Whose cruel Care restores my Sense and Pain,
For soon as I have Life I love again,
And with the fated softness strive in vain.
Distorted Nature shakes at the Controul,
With strong Convulsions rends my strugling Soul;
Each vital String cracks with th' unequal Strife,
Departing Love racks like departing Life;
Yet there the Sorrow ceases with the Breath,
But Love each day renews th' torturing scene of
       (Death.

          On

On the *death* of *dear* Statyra.

BEgone my Muse, Tears quench thy facre
                                    (Fire
True Grief, like Love, without thee can infpire.
Mod'rate Sorrows may be told with Art,
But the Diftractions of my troubled Heart
With fad Confufion I muft needs exprefs,
My Verfe will, like my Sighs, be numberlefs.
Ah, cruel Death! why was't thou fo fevere,
To take the Young, the Witty, and the Fair,
The gay *Satyra* in her blooming days:
Could no lefs Feaft ferve thy luxurious Jaws?
Would not the old or difcontented do?
Thofe whom Misfortune forc'd to wifh for you.
No thofe I by experience find you fly;   (muft dy.
And 'tis not thofe we would, but thofe you pleafe,
Guide me, fome Friend, if I have any one,
Whom Grief has fpar'd fince dear *Statyra*'s gone:
Lead me, I fay, to fome fad Cyprife fhade,
Dark as the Grave of the once lovely Maid;
There let me ever mourn the Friend I've loft:
Ye Gods, why was *Statyra* made a Ghoft?

                                           I can

On the death of dear Statyra.

Can no more gaze on that charming Face,
Hear that sweet Voice, nor have one dear Imbrace;
View that soft Air and Mien, and sport and play,
As we was wont on Summer-banks each day.
Ye pleasant Walks whom she so oft did grace,
Who's Charms did dart a Glory round the place.
Keep on your dismal Hue, let not the Spring
Put on your fresh Attire, nor Summer bring.
The less gay verdant Look ye Birds be still,
Sound not one Note unless sad *Philomel*.
Each lofty Tree hang down your stately Head,
Bud forth no more now gay *Statyra*'s dead;
But let your naked Boughs be ever join'd
In murmuring Sorrows with the sighing Wind:
No Blow, no Wind to move the yielding Bough,
My louder Sighs will do that Office now.
Keep back your force ye Springs that grace the
                                                           (Woods,
My Tears alone will swell you into Floods:
And all too little for the Friend I grieve,
Now she is gone 'tis not worth while to live.

On being —— tax'd with Symony.

Hence ye prophane Intruders, what d'e mean
To pry in secret Things that mayn't be seen
Your Pastor wonders at your Insolence,
'Tis Treason 'gainst your Ecclesiastick Prince.
Pulpits no more than Crowns must be prophan'd,
And if possess'd, not question'd how obtain'd:
With-hold your Hands, rend not the sacred Veil
Of his *Sanctorum*, lest his Priesthood fail.
The mighty Mysteries he so long conceal'd,
Will be by Lay-mens impious means reveal'd:
Sure, you'll not dare the Secret to pronounce,
No more than Jews their *Tetragrammatons*.
Yes, it is out the symonaick Sound,
With Horror doth the frighted Priest confound:
Sure, the last Trumpet can't amaze him more,
For he till then had set it on the Score;
In vain he'll to the Horns of th' Altar fly,
(*Alias* his Patron) for Security:
They'll drag him thence, that is no sacred Hold,
Since tip'd by him with symonaick Gold:
Had they been guided by the Patroness,
She kindly had contriv'd the Danger less:

No avaritious Zeal her Soul did move,
For she was nobly guided by her Love:
Thought Youth and Wit sufficient to prefer,
They were more tempting Things than Gold with (her.
But now the Favourite must his Purchase quit,
And live, not by his Learning, but his Wit.

An occasional Copy, in Answer to Mr. Joshua Barns, Extempore.

GO my proud Muse, yet thanks submisely yield,
   Not from obliging, but obliged Field;
Since mighty *Barns* doth Complement thee so,
The World will sure some little Pride allow.
He who's great Pen and elevated Sense,
Can grace the Acts of an Heroick Prince;
Yet condescends to celebrate thy Name,
Whose approbation is sufficient Fame.
What need was there to send it by a Friend?
Sure *Barns*'s Verse itself can recommend:
Sent by a Foe my Rage you had beguil'd,
And for its sake I had been reconcil'd.

How

A Song.

How should your Fancy be inrich'd by me,
Thou pregnant Author of best Poetry.
The fruitful Fields do stock the Barns each Year,
My barren Muse cannot allow it here:
She is but Poor, and been so long retir'd,
She could not write until by you Inspir'd.
Heaven has not giv'n Woman highest Wit,
But you good Nature to speak well of it;
I wish I did deserve the Praise you give,
Then like your Verse I should Immortal live;
But thus I take your Lines they speak to me,
Not what I am, but what I ought to be.

Song on Madam S——.

THO' the Amorous Beau,
  So courtly and fine,
  Admire a Dress,
  And Face of fifteen.

Let *Orinda* but speak,
Her Tongue will surprize,
And make him her Slave,
Spight of *Celia*'s bright Eyes.

The Fate.

Was she old and deform'd,
Her Wit and her Air,
Would conquer more Hearts,
Than the Young and the Fair.

Those Charms are more noble,
The Lovely and Kind
May vanquish the Body,
She conquers the Mind.

The Fate.

TEll me ye partial Power that wound our
(Hearts
Why strike ye not with sympathizing Darts?
Let Nymph and Swain be warm'd with equal Fires,
Not thus half-link Aversion and Desires.
Sure you delight to see us fondly crave
Those Joys, some other thankless Wretch must have:
Thus Love the sacred source of Unions crost,
And we perplex'd with what should please us most:
I would not rashly your Decrees prophane,
But am too much concern'd not to complain.

The Fate.

The wealthy *Strephon*'s panting at my Feet,
Tis I alone, that can his Joys compleat.
Yet with proud Scorn his dying Sighs repay,
Find all my Softness forc'd another way.
In gay *Exalis* centure all my Bliss,
Nor have a Thought but what's intirely his:
Careless of me, he does for *Cloe* pine,
Who slights him; and to *Damon* does resign.
Thus *Strephon* for *Larinda* almost dies,
But she can only soft *Exalis* prize,
He dotes on *Cloe*, she for *Damon* sighs.
Gods! tis too hard all Love yet all must part,
By some nice Touch turn every other Heart;
But if too cruel to redress us all,
To my *Exalis* let your Blessing fall.
On *Cloe* or *Larinda* the Change must be,
Grant I may please like her, or else she love like me;
For either way will ease my grateful Breast,
So our *Exalis* will but think he's blest.

A SONG.

HOW pleasant is Love,
  When forbid or unknown;
Was my Passion approv'd,
It would quickly be gone.

It adds to the Charms,
When we steal the Delight;
Why should Love be expos'd?
Since himself has no Sight.

In some Silvan Shade,
Let me sigh for my Swain;
Where none but an Eccho,
Will speak on't again.

Thus silent and soft,
I'll pass the Time on;
And when I grow weary,
I'll make my Love known.

On a Gentleman and his Wife visiting a Lady. He sleeping the while. Extempore *Spoke by* Morpheus.

PArdon, fair Nymph, I durst exert my Power,
Invade your Rights in a facetious Hour;
With gentle Slumbers seal those wondring Eyes,
That might, unweary'd on such Beauties gaze:
My Strength had fail'd had not your Forces joyn'd
And your own conquering Charms first struck him (blind
Your softer Graces did his Soul intrance,
Or I in vain should to the Sence advance.
All the Mysterious One I did not seize,
But spar'd that part which was most like to please,
She whose diverting Tongue could entertain,
With choice Collections from each Poet's Brain:
But see my Fetters could not bind him long,
He humbly sues for Pardon and a Song,
From your soft Voice which turns the Soul to Ear
And drousie as I am, I'll stay to hear:
If I with Nods should to the Tune keep time,
It is at worst, but a complaisant Crime:
Oh with what Joy! my Godhead I'd forsake,
Might you for ever Sing, and I for ever Wake.

The Vision.

Quite weary'd with the business of the Day,
  To unfrequented Shades I took my way,
And by a murmuring Stream supinely lay.
Soft thoughts confusedly revell'd in my Breast,
Till by composing Slumbers I was bless'd.
Hush't was my Sences as the unhaunted Grove,
And all the Vision of my Soul was Love;
Methoughts I saw a soft Celestial Youth,
Whose Eyes speak Love, and smiles Eternal Truth:
Gay as the Spring in all its vernal Pride,
With Amorous Joy sit panting by my side.
I gaz'd with Wonder at a Form so bright, (sight;
And thought some Sylvane God had bless'd my
With equal Scruple, Zeal and Passion mov'd,
If he should be ador'd or be belov'd.
His Eyes and Smiles darted refin'd delight,
As if Heavens glowing Glories touch'd the sight;
A thousand Charms his flowing Locks bestow,
For every Curl's inevitably so:
His welcome Head on my kind Bosom laid,
On a soft Flute delightful Airs he play'd.

Mean while such dear undoing looks he cast,
And every Note with artful Motions grac'd:
No Youth e'er seem'd so softning and Divine,
Sure he was made for Love, at least for mine.
Then was his Pipe out-rival'd by his Voice,
As when he Play'd all other Musick was:
A Mein so Gay and Shape that rivals *Joves*,
His Hand more soft than down of *Venus* Doves.
Her young *Adonis* had not half his Charms,
When he most pleasing fill'd her pressing Arms;
So kind he look'd, such tender things he said,
With eager Joy I grasp'd the lovely Shade.
The fleeting Charmer soon dissolv'd in Air,
I search'd around but could not find him there,
(Then to the Grove sigh'd Love and loud despair.)
It was *Alexis* form I did pursue,
My conscious Soul took the sad Omen too;
Cry'd out the lovely Youth forsakes my Breast,
And will be never but in Dreams possest.

The Power of Love.

IN this soft Amrous Age now Love is grown,
  The modish Entertainment of the Town,
And the fond Beau loves his half score aday,
The Ladies too almost as Vain as they;
Spare me, ye cruel Powers, let me not prove,
The only Victim of a lasting Love.
I had my share three tedious Years a Slave,
And knew no Joys but what *Phylaster* gave;
When spite of Vows he prov'd unjust at last,
In distant Shades contending Months I past,
Thought I could see the Youth at my return,
With gay Indifference and Unconcern.
I long'd to know the Temper of my Heart,
And see if Passion could outlive desert;
But this my Curiosity has won,
To know alas! I am again undone:
I thought my self with Resolution bless'd,
But the soft Gods came crouding to my Breast.
The sporting Boys delight in Amorous Pain,
And flock'd in hast to Revel here again;
With downy Wings they Fan the couchant Fire,
And every Spark revives with fresh desire:

To Marcella.

I Gaze and Sigh, and wish I'm just the same,
As the first Transports of my blooming Flame.
Almighty Love thy Power to me is known,
Without new Tortures I'll thy Godhead own;
But if I'm doom'd to Love may my Fate be,
(Rather than him) to love each Face I see.
'Tis Sin against the custom of the Nation,
To love but one and all this while with Passion,
I'd rather be the shifting Fool in Fashion.
Then if I'm tortur'd with Variety,
I shan't be blam'd for Nonconformity.

To Marcella.

IN this so wanton and debaucht an Age,
  We come to find out Virtue on the Stage;
By a promiscuous Choice it can't be done,
Our nicer Fate compels to You alone.
You, who's triumphant Virtue doth declare,
That Women can withstand the fatal Snare
Of vast Temptation, when she's Young and Fair.
In you the ancient Miracle we see,
(Tho' here we can boast but of One to Three)
                              Unhurt

To Marcella.

Unhurt amidst the mighty Flames you move,
The wond'ring Gazers only Martyrs prove;
Of all your Sex Great *Albion* must prefer
You the chast *Lucrece* of her Theater.
Ye yielding Nymphs now you have no excuse,
Nor blame the Beaus you did your Honour lose;
For your Defence your softness is exprest
With (oh such Charms! no Woman can resist).
Yes Woman can in this fair Maid we see,
Contempt of all their Love and Gallantry;
Wit, Youth and Beauty, does this Lady bless,
She's made for Love and fitted for Address:
While Crowds of Slaves ly sighing at her Feet,
She bravely scorns what you would run to meet.
Among them all doubtless there's more than One,
Charming as those by whom you were undone:
The Soft, the Gay, the Great, the knowing Man,
Have try'd all ways Wit, Wealth, or Passion can,
To gain this Fair who still her Heart secures,
Unmov'd she stands, slights all their soft Amours,
What would you give the Scene of Love were
(yours?

I know your Spite imputes it to her Pride,
Be't what it will her Honours justify'd:
Her Virtue is the greater Miracle,
To stand with that by which the Angels fell.

Hail,

The Invocation.

Hail, lovely Maid, who contradicts the times,
Your Virtue wears a Vail like others Crimes:
How do your Eyes and Tongue bely your Heart,
When languishing you play the amorous part,
And softly fold your seeming loving Arms,
And speak and look a thousand killing Charms?
Fair, soft Deceiver, oh! were I the Men,
I'd give the World you was in earnest then;
Your pleas'd Spectators with such Joys you bless,
They wish your Virtues or your Charms were less.

The Invocation.

With some auspicious Aid ye Pow'rs above,
Help to support the weight of slighted Love.
I ask not Rage to curse the daring Man;
That by Instinctive Power all Women can,
But keep me mild as when Love first began.
'Tis the malignancy of low desire,
That with neglect turns to revengeful Fire:
But my great Passion, like Æthereal Flame,
Without Supply can ever burn the same;
Love glows in every Atom of my Frame:

Sparkles

The Invocation.

Sparkles in every Thought, flames at my Heart,
Like the extensive Soul it does exert ;
'Tis all in all, and all in every part.
 From his cold Breast no languid warmth I want,
His Fires when at their height to mine are faint,
Yet my hard Fate forces this soft Complaint.
That so much Truth is unreguarded lost,
And we have least when we deserve it most.
Oh ! was I fickle as the restless Wind,
Or as the wiser part of Woman-kind :
Then for the Charmer I'd no longer mourn,
But treat his Negligence with equal Scorn.
He should no more my slighted Favours wear,
But from the sighing Crowd that deaf my Ear,
I'd choose some kinder Youth and fix 'em there.
But oh ! my tender Soul too weak does prove,
Either to change or bear the force of Love ;
Too sure 'tis doom'd by my relentless Fate
That I must love and sink beneath the weight.

On the Author of Religion by Reason, or the Light of Nature a Guide to Divine Truth.

Hail, modest Author, who obscure do'st lie,
   But to prevent our fond Idolatry;
Thou'st baffl'd all the Writers of the Age,
Who's active Pens reach the ten thousandth Page:
And doth commit with so much Industry,
Their Names in Folio to Posterity.
Who's wire drawn Notions and expanded Sense,
Swell a great Volume with as great Expence;
Which when we've read the whole Prolix design,
Contains not half that's in one Page of thine.
Nay, choose the best in thy small Tract we see,
A thousand of them in Epitome;
Our way of Study is by Contemplation,
Revolving Thoughts in the mind by dull Sucession
But yours seems Angel-like pure Intuition.
To what perfections Orthography brought,
How could you write in Words so like your
Truths so Divine in so refin'd a Stile, (Thought;
Sure Angels view with a consenting Smile:

Let

On Atheism.

Let the bold Atheist read thy Noble Line,
In every Leaf he'll see a Power Divine.
Not long Disputes confounding the intent,
But subtle clear convincive Argument;
Had *Hobs* but seen it, that bold daring Man,
Himself had burnt his own Leviathan.
What sceptick Scruples can in Man be rais'd,
But by your Conquering Truths may be appeas'd?
The *Persian* Sophi and the papal Chair,
Usurp what Heaven doth sure on you confer.
The careful Student need not any more,
Waste Purse and Time to turn great Volumes o'er,
Your well fraught Book in which all Truths agree,
Will be itself sufficient Library.

On Atheism.

TELL me, ye daring Atheist, what's your End,
To what sure Point do your Debauches tend?
You would be happy and secure it here,
And have no Glymps of future Worlds appear;
Your Minds scarce doubt, but Crimes Reversion (fear.
Who

On Atheism.

Whoever knew a sober Atheist yet?
Tis the Extravagance of floating Wit,
Buoy'd up with Wine and sensual Apetite.
That Wine can uncreate by all's confest,
Unmakes the Man, and levels him with Beast:
What is't they would not give the Change were true?

For they with Doubts do all their Crimes pursue;
They are more plagu'd to curb the Thoughts of (Hell,
Then all the Self-Denials to live well.
No Man at first to Atheism inclin'd,
He takes that Refuge after he has sin'd;
Bold in his Crimes untill he can't repent,
Then strives to think there is no Punishment:
Lull'd in lewd Pleasures from Devotion free,
We call him Atheist, *Alias* Debauchee.
Where is the Happiness they so much boast,
Their Joys are in their Consequences lost?
Women and Wine their greatest dear Concern,
But cheat their Hopes and make an ill Return;
Raptur'd with Charms of his deluding Fair,
Oh! the Delights and Bliss he centers there;
And in carouzing with lascivious Songs,
And all the Frolicks which to Wine belongs.

These

On Atheism   63

These are their *Summum Bonum*, here they're bless'd,
In those wild Joys that sting while they'r possess'd;
Their Disappointments Pride and Jealousy,
Are more severe than Fast and Mortify;
A hectoring Rival or Decease at last,
Fully revenge the gay Delight that's past;
The **Pains** and **Qualms** that wait a drunken Fit,
Severely scourge the Gust of Appetite;
They're punish'd here, and if there is no Hell,
(As they would fain believe but cannot tell.)
We have the best on't for we're Happy now,
Our Joys no torturing Excess allow;
Pleas'd and secure amidst our Bliss we move,
And with just Transports hope for more above;
In this we're bless'd, and since it lasts as long
As Life, what matter tho' we'er in the wrong?
We'er Happy whilst we are, and shall not know
If we mistake, whether we did or no;
If you'r in th' wrong, your Error more perplex'd,
You'r plagu'd in this World to be damn'd i'th' next,

On

On a Sermon Preach'd Sept. *the* 6*th,* 1697. *on these Words,* You have sold your selves for Nought.

WIth *Grotius* on *New-Testament* yo've done,
And chose Authentick *Coke* and *Littleton*;
The latters Tenures did inspire your Brain,
To vent your self in legislative Strain:
Where you each nice Distinction did pursue,
The Bargain, Sale, and the *habendum* too.
It was not done by Lease or Mortgage then,
To be redeem'd as you told how and when;
By Deed of Feoffment we had passed away,
For nothing too our Tenement of Clay;
And that the Devil who the Purchase bought,
He nothing gave nor nothing had he got.
On this you Cant (awhile) at last recal,
Cum Pertinentiis, he had gotten all;
When of the Gospel you make Law take Place,
Statues may well get upper-hand of Grace:
Sure you the Primitive design have mist,
Joshua must yield to an Evangelist.
But *Littleton* in you has got the start,
Did'st know if thou in Church or Temple were't?
Tho'

Tho' you so Zealously the *Non-cons* hate,
Methinks too like the *Pro* and *Cons* you Prate,
The Sermon is at best but a Debate:
Instead of Proofs you bring us Presidents,
Need more the Judges than the Saints consents.
You Declare, Plead, Join Issue or Demur,
Then fell at last with (*come ceo Sur* ;)
Fatal Defeazance, for if you Preach so,
Your Hearers may remain in *Statu quo*:
So far you on the legal Rights intrench,
We scarcely know your Pulpit from the Bench.

A SONG.

WHen first I saw *Laurinda*'s Face,
   I bless'd the dear Surprize,
For there was sporting every Grace;
Love wanton'd in her Eyes.

A thousand ways she has to move,
Not Looks and Smiles alone,
Her Shape and Mien might Conquer *Jove*;
And make the God her own.

But oh! the Fair displays her Charms,
For Conquest, not Delight;
Proudly denies those lovely Arms,
To which her Eyes invite.

On my leaving S——y.

S——y thou dearest soft Retreat adieu
Methink I tremble at the leaving you;
You, whose safe Harbour kindly did receive,
My Shipwrack'd Vessel and gave means to live:
With Gilded Stern and Gaudy Sails I mov'd,
Fraught with this Wish, be Great and be Belov'd,
My Pageant Bark undauntedly I steer'd,
No Rocks nor Wind, nor Enemies I fear'd:
Young and unskill'd in this unlucky Sea,
For want of Ballast, Storms did ruin me.
That blast of Hell, rude spiteful Pop'ler breath,
Tore all my Sails and threaten'd sudden Death;
There was no casting Anchor in this Storm,
That was but Ruin in another Form:
For hope was all the lading I could boast,
Thus was I most inevitably lost.

On my leaving S——y.

Left to the Mercy of the faithless Winds,
My tatter'd Bark no friendly shelter finds;
Till some kind Star dear S——y mark'd out thee,
For her repairer and security.
'Tis true, thou couldst not fit her out again,
With Masts and Tackling for the mighty Main;
But as a Pleasure-Boat in thy smooth Streams,
(Happy defect that keeps from such extreams,)
Where no rough Winds but a safe Oar commands,
And if I please at each bless'd Shade she Lands.
There on a verdant Bank I set me down,
Contemn persuit of Passion and Renown:
At all my former daring Follies smile,
And bless the Storms that blow'd me to this Isle;
The Fortunate to me, and doth contain,
Those solid Joys, I elsewhere sought in vain.
But ah! the Fates again do summon me,
To the loath'd Ocean Popularity;
Guard me ye Gods with this one Bliss alone,
Tho' I am seen, yet let me not be known.

The Gratitude.

MY injur'd Love, thy Anthems ceaſe awhile,
And hear my Vows with an accepting (Smile.
By thee I ſwear, by thee as ſacred now,
I'll pay thee all the Paſſion that I owe.
Forgive, that I ſo negligent did prove,
Was ſuch a careleſs Debtor to thy Love:
As ſome wild Gallant who profuſely ſpends
That on his Frolicks, which ſhould pay his Friends;
Yet gives good Words, is complaiſant and kind,
And with ſmall Preſents ſhews his thankful Mind.
So did I manage my vaſt ſtock of Love,
Did neither juſt, nor yet ungrateful prove;
Heaven knows, to pay thee all I had begun,
But the neglected Score too far had run.
Fatal Delay, for now the dreadful Sum,
I with kind Horror offer at thy Tomb;
What'er I ow'd thy Life, I'll pay thy Duſt,
Bring all th' Arrears of Paſſion, and be Juſt;
Accept it now, altho alas too late,
And pity this ſad Preſſure of my Fate.

Thou

The Gratitude.

Thou wer't so pleas'd with what thou hadst below,
'Twould raise thy Bliss could'st thou my Passion know,
That's great and lasting as thy Joys are now.
Not the least Thought shall to ought else be given,
I offer all to thee, and what retains thee, Heaven.
Tho' at thy Death no sable Scenes of State,
Nor solemn Pageantry did gild thy Fate;
No pompous Griefs of a Mechanick Throng
Of hir'd Mourners usher'd thee along;
Nor gaudy Scutchion daub'd thy early Herse,
Yet 'twas adorn'd with thy *Clarinda*'s Verse:
One moment's Grief of mine is of more Cost,
Than a Majestick thirty Days can boast.
Those pageant Sorrows on the Dead bestow'd,
But touch the Fancy of the gazing Croud,
Where scarce one Tear in earnest is allow'd.
Amidst a thousand torturing Pangs I live,
Too well I know, both who and how to grieve.
It is more Honour to be mourn'd by me.
Than all their stately dark Solemnity,
Whose Riches purchase a forc'd Obsequey.
Tho' on thy Grave no Statue I erect,
Yet the smooth Stone shall with my Tears be deck'd,

No, take a Tomb more fitting thy Defert,
Yes, I'll infhrine thee in my generous Heart.
So far for thee a *Niobe* I'm grown,
That now 'tis fitting for that Ufe alone.
No Monument more glorious or fafe,
Grac'd with a vital crimfon Epitaph.
My bleeding Heart fhall this Infcription give,
Not here you Lie, but here for ever Live.

On my wedding Day.

Abandon'd Day, why doft thou now appear?
Thou muft no more thy wonted Glories (wear;
Oh! Rend thy felf out of the circling Year.
With me thou'rt ftript of all thy pompous Pride,
Art now no feftival Caufe, I no Bride:
In thee no more muft the glad Mufick found,
Nor pleafing Healths in chearful Bowls go round,
But with fad Cyprefs drefs'd, not Mirtle crown'd;
Ne'er grac'd again with joyful Pageantry:
The once glad Youth that did fo honour thee
Is now no more; with him thy Triumph's loft,
He always own'd thee worthy of his Boaft.

Such

On my Wedding Day.

Such Adorations he still thought thy due,
I learn'd at last to celebrate thee too;
Tho' it was long e're I could be content,
To yield you more than formal Complement;
If my first Offering had been Free-Will,
I then perhaps might have enjoy'd thee still:
But now thou'rt kept like the first mystick Day,
When my reluctant Soul did Fate obey,
And trembling Tongue with the sad Rites com-
(ply'd,
With timerous Hand th' amazing Knot I ty'd,
While Vows and Duty check'd the doubting Bride.
At length my reconcil'd and conquer'd Heart,
When 'twas almost too late own'd thy Desert,
And wishes thou wast still, not that thou never
(wer't?
Wishes thee still that celebrated Day,
I lately kept with sympathizing Joy.
But Ah! thou now canst be no more to me,
Than the sad Relick of Solemnity;
To my griev'd Soul may'st thou no more appear,
Be blotted out of Fate's strict Calender.
May the Sun's Rays ne'er be to thee allow'd,
But let him double every thick wrought Cloud,
And wrap himself in a retiring Shroud;

The Fatality.

Let unmixt Darkness shade the gloomy Air,
Till all our sable Horizon appear,
Dismale as I, black as the Weeds I wear;
With me thy abdicated State deplore,
And be like me, that's by thy self no more.

The Fatality.

COME all ye grand Predestinarians now,
Your Doctrine to the Height I will allow:
I who with utmost Force resist my Fate,
But am to Ills alone predestinate;
In vain I strive th' immutable Decree,
Has pass'd on my unlucky Destiny.
With Sighs and Tears I did at first begin,
To conquer Fate as others would their Sin;
Each Path I trod I went with Caution on,
But every Step doth lead to be undone:
And when a threatening Storm was in my View,
I from it (wisely as I thought) withdrew;
But whilst the approaching Ills with Fear I shun,
Into some other certain Harms I run;
So when some mighty Grief did press my Soul,
I would th' uneasy Tyranny controul;
(Like

The Fatality.

(Like a distracted Man that will not bear,
Those Fetters which Discretion makes him wear;
But frets and raves, and breaks the friendly Chain,
Which did from greater Injuries restrain;
He'll not be bar'd a dangerous Liberty,
Tho' he to Outrages and Mischief fly.)
Thus I from one Misfortune force my Way,
By Means that does to greater still betray;
One Sorrow seldom attends long on me,
I have a torturing Variety,
I change and change, yet still 'tis Misery.
A Hydra Fate my Ruin does pursue,
Cut off one ill, strait, there springs up a new,
And they'll arise *ad infinitum* too.
Ther's none the mystick Scrolls of Fate can read,
Nor shun the Ills by mighty Powers decreed,
Hood-wink'd by them, just as they guide we tread.
In vain we say we this or that will do,
It cannot be unless they'll have it so;
The only Way to ease our Discontents,
Is to conclude they must be such Events;
Such as the mighty hidden source of Things,
Bubbles from it's inevitable Springs,

An Ode on the Death of Mr. Dryden.

I.

AS when *Plebeans* at a Monarch's death,
    (Which seems Prophan'd by Sighs from
                           vulgar Breath;)
With sawcy Grief pity the helpless Fate
Of what they fear'd, almost ador'd of late.
So I the meanest that did e'er aspire,
To own herself of the Muses Empire;
Who scarcely can my Tribute pay,
To acknowledge their Imperial sway.
With arrogant, yet conscious Grief, presume,
To shed a Tear on their Vice-gerents awful Tomb;
Ah! who'd have thought that seeming deathless
    With every Art and Grace indow'd;   (Man,
Should have a Life, but of the usual Span,
    And shrink into a common Shroud.
But his unequall'd worth can never dy,
    Nothing can e'er his matchless Laurels blast,
Tho' *Albion*'s self should be destroy'd and wast;
    And in forgotten Ruins lie.

An Ode on the Death, &c.

The ecchoing Trump of Fame his Glories will re-
To all the wondering Universe, (reherse,
Till it Joyn sound with the Tremendious last.

II.

Sure Poets are not made of common Earth,
Or he at least may boast a nobler Birth;
Each Atom with soft Numbers was inspir'd,
And flowing Fancy with one lasting Rapture fir'd:
Altho' the mighty Secret's not disclos'd,
He surely was like *Thebes* with artful Tunes com-
The Voices of the sweet melodious Nine, (pos'd,
   In Consort joyn'd *Apollo*'s forming Lyre,
   Did thousand purest particles Inspire;
With tuneful Measures Harmony Divine.
At the sacred commanding Sound,
With Animation passing vulgar Souls,
The knowing willing Atoms came,
None the creative Strains controuls;
But by energy of Ayrs Divine compound,
The almost omniscient Frame.

And

And for a Soul which scarce was wanting here,
  In all the pre-existing Magazine,
    Not one was seen ;
Worthy in thy alloted Glories to appear.
No great *Apollo*'s self, with his own Rays,
(For nothing less could the bright Form improve,
Infus'd celestial Sapience from above ;
  To qualify thee for immortal Bays.

III.

Apollo once before a sacred Structure blest,
Where all the Inquisitive World did come,
  For an ambiguous Doom ;
And splendid Pomp amaz'd the curious Guest.
Yet with less Glory did at *Delphos* shine,
When floors of Marble, roofs of Gold,
Did his oraculous God-head hold ;
  Then in thy living Shrine,
There fetter'd with a sacerdotal Yoke,
Uncheckt in thee, the God has always spoke.
In thee no less Magnificent appears,
Nor with less Splender did his Power exert,
Then when above a Soveraign sway he bears ;
In Learning Poetry, and every Godlike Art.

But

ut oh! the Deity is silenc'd now, (flow,
'o more celestial Cadence from thy Tongue will
nd all the lesser Fanes with Grief expire,
    All gasping ly,
  With fainting Groans deplore,
    Great *Dryden* is no more;
    And with declining Fire
ling their own Requiem in thy Obsequie.
  Farewel to Inspiration now,
  All sacred extacies of Wit,
    The softer Excellence,
Of melting Words and rapturing Sence,
Ye will no more with Divine Sweetness flow;
    But Poetry submit
  To the bold Enthusiastick Rage
Of a deserted and malicious Age.

IV.

Only the Pythagorean Faith we doubt,
Else if thy great Soul should transmigrated be,
    It might be parcell'd out
And stock each Age with Laureats till Eternity.

                              Ah!

An Ode on the Death

Ah! Where is thy harmonious Spirit now?
Teaching softer Numbers to the Sphears,
Or makes some Star with greater Lustre glow,
Or roamest in the extended Space thy long Eter-
(nity of Years
No, to th' sacred softer Shades thou'rt gone,
The Souls of Poets needs must thither fly;
(I'm sure they Lovers live how e're they die.)
But thou so many Laurels here hast won,
   As plants a new *Elizium* of thy own.
Triumphant sit beneath th' immortal Shade,
Of ever blooming Wreaths which less than those
That are below for softest Lovers made. (will fade,
Therefore the *Mantuan* Swain need not retreat,
   But keep his antient Regal Seat;
Which else at thy Approach he would resign,
For well he knows Wit's sacred Throne is thine:
See he with Thanks salutes thy skilful Hand,
   Which so successfully has taught;
His long fram'd Works the Language of our Land,
With Art in every Line, and Grace in every Thought.
   None their intrinsick Value can deny,
   The well plac'd Pride of antient *Rome*,
Polish'd by thee is now our Boast become;
Sparkling with all the Glories of true Poetry,
Receives from all a just and happier Doom.
                                        Orpheus

Orpheus and all the tuneful Poets there,
With Joys new dated celebrate thy Fame,
   In an eternal soft celestial Air ; (slighted Name.
For all the Honours thou hast done the so long

V.

And we whom thou hast left behind,
   Are all employ'd about thee too ;
Altho thy Worth too great a Theme we find,
At least our Gratitude in Grief we show.
Our best Encomiums but prophane thy Name,
Unless successful *Congreves* artful Line ;
   That only Rival of so great a Fame,
   Can Justice do to thine.
My well meant *Trophy* blushing I must rear,
Unkind *Melpomene* affords no Aid,
Tho' I so often beg'd and pray'd,
My softer Voice she would not hear.
Amongst the mighty Men she's busie now,
Tis they I find best charm immortal Females too;
Tho' she'll not teach how I shall Numbers keep,
My Admiration in Heroick's dress,
Or in a softer Ode my Griefs express,
Tis my own Fault being Woman, if I fail to weep.
Since this great Man insatiate Fate obey'd,
How is Wit's Empire lessen'd and decay'd ?   It

It scarce a Province now appears,
  Come then let's joyn our Tears;
  Cease not till an Ocean flow,
Twine round the Muses Plat, till it an Island grow,
There let's possess her constant Joys,
   Spite, Poverty and Noise.
  Tho' bounded safe with a *Castalian* Sea,
They ne'er must hope their Isles the Fortunate will
(be.

The Advice.

I.

PEace, busie Soul, let distant Things alone,
   Only the present Time's thy own;
  Leave to the Gods what shall hereafter be,
  Forbear the Search of dark Futurity.
If thou'lt at once more than one Minute live,
  Thou must design or dread or grieve;
  In turning back Remembrance represents,
     Black Images of Discontent.

What

The Advice.

What happen'd to torment a Year ago,
Altho' it really ceases to do so?
If thou will't ruminate, 'tis still A Woe.
 Thus what is past will always present be,
  And in Idea ever torture thee;
  On Pleasures too if we reflect,
 They have the same unkind Effect;
  We are as angry they are past,
As at those Griefs which we compel to last:
But tell me, partial Soul, ah tell me why?
Things of such Contrariety,
In thy Revolves should be the same to thee.

II.

One deep obliterating Draught of Lethe take,
Blot all the torturing Records out;
Yet then thou'lt not be bless'd I doubt,
  But nice Inquiries make.
  Yes, the forbidden Book of Fate,
Thou needs must pry into with curious Eyes,
By'ts unintelligible Lines thy Actions state, (Wise.
Where nothing's plain unless the Curse of being
Now Form great threatning Monsters in thy Brain,
Then rack thy Skill to have the Phantoms slain;

The Advice.

In the safe present Scene thou wilt not rest,
 But in remoter Things be bless'd.
This or that distant Joy propose,
And much of Life extravagantly lose,
In Search of what Fate will elsewhere dispose.
Thy Plots and Forecasts thou conceiv'st in vain,
 Links of th' inevitable Chain;
 Short-sighted Soul thou canst not see,
 What shall to Morrow be,
Yet wilt indulge thy fruitless Curiosity.
So some unlucky Engineer
Does all the fit Materials compound,
That are in Art or Nature found;
Will glorious Fire-Works prepare.
(Fancies he sees his various Comets rise, (the Skys;)
Outshine and mount up to their radiant likeness in
Thinks they will satisfie his Pride and Cost,
 But ah! he hopes in vain.
For almost finish'd ere he is aware,
A Spark by chance lights in the Train,
And all with one afrighting Blaze is in confusion lost.

III.

Since thou, my Soul, must grieve or bafl'd be,
 For once be rul'd by me;
 No more reflect,
No more with studious Care project,
 Nor look beyond thy present Destiny.

The Advice.

I charge thee ne'er contrive no more,
Thou'lt fare no better than thou didst before;
With *Ixion*'s mistaken Joys prepare,
Thy fond Embrace for the delusive Air;
So often fool'd ne'er hope to win at last,
Thy future Doom's stamp'd with thy Past.
Then Fate doth seem with her own Hand,
To lead to the self-promis'd Land;
Yet e'er our weary'd Steps reach the long wish'd
Storms and Darkness doth surround, (for Ground,
And the gay Prospect can no more be found.
Tho' we by chance (a mighty Chance indeed,)
Should to our selves propose what is decreed:
Yet to my Cost this Truth I've learn'd,
With passive Ease we should be unconcern'd:
For Fate of our Designs no Use will make,
But her own mysterious Methods take.
Then why do we perplex our selves in vain,
For what we know not how to get, or whether
(we must gain?

IV

Then live to Day, design nor fear no more,
Nor grieve upon a former Score:
What was once is gone,
And that which we expect may ne'er come on.
Those who on Yesterdays and Morrows live,
Neglect what Heaven does really give;

    Which only is the present Day,
And that in fleeting Moments posts away;
    Let me enjoy each Minute then,
Not starve to Day, to feast I know not when;
    Since the full Glass at the inviting Lip,
    From the too cautious Hand may slip.
    Give me ye Gods my Blessings now,
On th' expecting Man your future Gifts bestow.
    They who the present Hour neglect,
    Because an other better they expect:
    Useful Estates do pass away,
        For future Pay;
    Are always Creditors to Fate,
    And she too often pays too late;
There's none but Fools procrastinate.

To Thyrsis *on his* Pastoral *to Mr.* Creech.

COme all ye tender Nymphs and sighing Swains,
    Hear how our *Thyrsis*, *Daphnis* death com-
                                           (plain
In Notes more sweet he doth his Sorrows tell,
Than the harmonious mournful *Philomel*.

Pastoral on Mr. Creech.

With his sad Airs let all our Griefs combine,
And sighing Eccho in the Consort joyn;
Till o'er the pittying Plains the Tidings spread,
Pans Darling *Daphnis* to *Eliziums* fled:
Daphnis the tunefull'st Youth we knew among,
The softening Swains till gentle *Thyrsis* Sung.
Thyrsis, whose Muse of all our blooming Grove,
Best pities Lovers and best Sings of Love;
Soft are thy Lines as the first tender Fire,
That warms the Breast e'er it commence Desire:
Thy moving Numbers all our Passions share,
Sigh, Languish, Weep, Just what we read we are.
By the soft Magick rais'd to Extacy,
With *Daphnis* love, and with him too we dy;
Had he addrest but in thy melting Strain,
(And he could do it, sure if any Swain.)
The Nymph in spite of her presuming Charms,
With Joy had yeilded to his wishing Arms.
Impatient Youth, that Death itself could bear,
Rather than scorns of the neglecting Fair:
But thus we fondly Rave to miss the Joy,
Love natural as Life, does Life destroy.
To Wit alone Passion does fatal prove,
Fools may be lew'd but know not how to Love;

Since it in learn'd Breasts such Woes create,
Thyrsis taking warning by great *Daphnis* Fate:
But to your Charms Caution does needless seem,
Fear less Love, on you need not dye like him.
For oh! what Nymph could e'er so stupid prove,
As not to melt if *Thyrsis* Name but Love?
What pity 'twas the learn'd *Daphnis* dy'd,
The slighted Victim of a Virgins Pride.
Had'st thou been silent, it more Tears had cost,
Now half our Grief's in Admiration lost;
So well you Mourn the Shepherd's amorous Fate,
In such soft strains his sad fond Fall relate.
Pan would himself quit Immortality,
To be in Death so sweetly Sung by thee.

Delia *to* Phraartes *on his Playing* Cæsar Borgia.

IF *Cæsar* from his *Stygian* Coast could come,
   To see you Play, he'd bless his former Doom;
Pleas'd with the promis'd Glories which he lost,
And in your Form, confess the greater Boast.

Had

Playing Cæsar Borgia.

Had he been bless'd but with your soft Address,
His Love had never known such ill Success;
That Godlike Mein and that seraphick Voice,
Would have compell'd nice *Bellamira*'s choice.
Had half your Charms in the true *Borgia* been,
We ne'er his mourning Tragedy had seen.
You'r so Divine, that Heavens peculiar care,
Would so much Gallantry and Sweetness spare.
In vain Historians and Poets too,
To such brave Men celestial Honous do,
They ne'er seem Gods, till personated by you.
A rugged Virtue and the chance of War,
Did bless their Hero's with that Character;
The Antiquated Shade the Poets seize,
And tune the Soul to what a pitch they please:
With artful Notes they grace each noble Line,
But your soft touch gives it an air Divine.
What pains they take for Praise while you with ease,
Transport with that which they scarce hop'd could
(please?

Th' Imperial *Cæsars* when with Fortune bless'd,
In all their gay triumphant splendor drest,
And more than Royal State thro' *Rome* they rode,
(Both prais'd and fear'd and thought almost a God,

88 *To* Clarona *drawing* Alexis's
When fetter'd Kings did grace the Victory,)
Mid'st all their dazling Pomp look'd less than thee.
If Gods their Glories would expose to view,
To joy Mankind they'd look and speak like you.

To Clarona *drawing* Alexis's *Picture and presenting it to me.*

THE curious noble Present which you make,
I with surprize and conscious Blushes take.
Why was the gay *Alexis* made your choice,
Has he my private or my publick Voice?
My nicer Temper cannot that allow,
Tho' you have gone the way to make him so;
Some other Friend would equal Thanks command,
Tho' he was fittest for your skilful Hand:
As the best Poets who's Art Rivals thine,
Should always choose a Subject that's Divine.
I must confess th' obligingness of Fate,
To let you see him tho' he never sate;
A fair Idea form'd in your great Mind,
You ventur'd on, and 'twas as you design'd:

'Twas

'Twas the gay Youth in all his conquering Charms,
As might seduce a *Daphne* to his Arms.
His Smiles, his Eyes, his Air each lovely Grace,
All that our Sex can wish in any Face;
It was exactly him, and yet 'twas more,
An Art which none did e'er express before:
Should Nature strive for Ostentation sake,
And would another bright *Alexis* make,
'Twould be less like than what is done by thee,
She'd blushing throw her long us'd Pencil see;
Nay, you blest Painters this advantage give,
Beyond what is allow'd to those that live.
With sublimated Art you Time subdue, (too.
Draw Charms to th' Life and make them lasting
Now fam'd *Apelles* from thy Throne look down,
And see a female Hand outdo thy own.
The Piece which unaccomplish'd was by thee,
The just Despair of long Posterity,
By her may with advantage finisht be.
The mighty Task can only be her Right,
Who so exactly draws at casual sight:
I with proud Joy the lovely Present take,
Both for *Alexis* and *Clarona*'s sake.
My two best Friends, Illustrious now appear,
A pleasing Form drawn by a Hand so fair;

Charm'd

Charm'd by your Art, I generously consent,
To own 'tis my Delight as well as Ornament.

A SONG.

A Thousand Gay obliging Youths,
   I unconcern'd can see,
But when *Exalis* doth appear;
   He shakes my Constancy.

   In spite of all my Proud Resolves,
I soften at his Charms,
And almost wish my self to be;
   In his regardless Arms.

   Some milder Power, reverse my Fate,
He's doom'd to Love elsewhere,
I beg my Passion you'd Translate;
   I would not rob his Fair.

   Let him persue his fond Amour,
Grant I may pity those,
Who sigh for me and make him kind;
   Unto the Nymph he's chose.

Erato

Erato *the Amorous Muse on the Death of* John Dryden, *Esq.*

IN the wisht Close of Evening's welcome gloom,
My longing steps reacht an inviting Bloom;
Whose untrod Paths the sadning Cypress grac't,
And in small Plats were softer Myrtles plac't.
The lofty Cedars with extended Arms,
Twine to keep off the force of roughest Storms;
And numerous tow'ring Arbourets they made,
The solemn Glory of the pleasing Shade:
On verdant Moss, Nature's rich cloth of State,
By a clear thrilling Stream supine I sate:
Upon my Hand my thoughtful Head reclin'd,
Sad soft Ideas entertain'd my Mind,
And I to *sing* some Lovers fate inclin'd;
But strait *Erato*, whom I did invoke,
Forbid my Choice, her Speech abruptly broke,
At last in Sighs the Interdiction spoke.
Ye shall no more write tender moving Strains,
To please the Nymphs and melt the wishing Swains
But to the World my Sorrows you shall tell,
How I have *griev'd* since the lost Heroe fell,
My darling *Dryden* whom I lov'd so well.

He

He who has done such Glories to my Name,
Immortal as my self has made my Fame;
Watchful as Lovers I first saw his Fate
With raging Sounds *Parnassus* loss relate.
Call'd all my Sisters with my frantick Cries,
And every God to *Join* in th' Obsequies,
With Tears made *Helycon* brackish as the Seas.
Like a deserted Maid in Wild Despair,
I tore my Myrtle Wreath and flowing Hair,
My Mantle rent and shatter'd in the Air;
Then in loose Cypriss vail'd *my* useless Charms,
Sight till I turn'd our *Æther* into Storms.
No more I'll wanton on our Mountains brow,
Nor curious Pains upon my Locks bestow;
In amorous Folds my Rosey Mantle twine,
And sooth soft Languishments in airs Divine:
But careless throw me in some dusky Shade,
Which Willows, Cypress, Yew has awful made,
There to my Votress Eccho I'll complain,
Whose Complaisance reverberates again,
My piercing Groans thro' every Wood and Plain.
Thus I and she in *an* Eternal round,
Will my celestial Griefs for *Dryden*'s Death resound.
Dryden, who with such Ardour did invoke,
That I thro' him my greatest Raptures spoke.

Whis-

Whisper'd a thousand tender melting Things,
Till he writ Lays moving as *Orpheus* strings.
Oft I for Ink did radiant *Nectar* bring,
And gave him Quills from infant *Cupid*'s Wing:
Whose gentle force did as Victorious prove,
As if they'd been th' immortal Shafts of Love.
Warm'd every Breast with a surprizing Fire,
And in the nicest tenderest Thoughts inspire;
Such Lustre still grac't his magnetick Line,
It was both Irresistless and Divine.
With what celestial Cadence doth he tell,
The pristine Joys of Love, e'er Mankind fell;
When in the blooming Grove the first kind Pair,
With amorous Sighs fan'd the ambrosial Air:
Smiling on flowry Banks supinely laid,
The ardent Youth prest the unblushing Maid.
In his soft Lines such Extacies they Boast,
To hear *their* loves Rivals the Bliss they lost;
When *Cleopatra*'s Passion he adorns,
How Nobly *Anthony* the Empire scorns:
Dissolv'd in her kind Arms transported lay,
For Love's soft Joy, gave the rough Crown away.
Such Realms of Bliss the Hero there possest,
Sighing fond Vows on her returning Breast;

Who reads their Languishments their Passions feel
Intranc't in Joys too exquisite to tell.
When an incestuous Flame his Theme has been,
He almost *charms* us to forgive the Sin.
My favourite *Ovid's* strains I did improve,
And taught my *Dryden* tenderer *Arts* of Love;
Such Arts had our addressing *Phœbus* known,
Daphne, tho' coy, had not Unconquer'd flown,
But brought the Hero forth, and not their Crown.
He so advanc'd whatever I bestow'd,
I was Love's Muse, but he himself the God.

Delia *to* Phraartes *on his mistake of three Ladies writing to him.*

SAY, noble Youth, thou Glory of the Stage,
  Gay soft Delight of the admiring Age;
What would'st thou give thou didst thy *Delia* know,
Or that the Nymph who writ the Billet Deau,
Could have oblig'd you with Heroicks too?
To purchase your Esteem they all agreed,
And tho' one Scroul, 'twas a Tripartite Deed.

Methinks in you I royal *Paris* see,
Like him employ'd ill suiting your Degree;
In his Disguise he rural Conquests won,
But you brave Youth have greater Wonders done;
Your Power by neither Sex can be withstood,
Your own are all oblig'd and ours subdu'd
Wit Fortune, Beauty for your Voice contest,
Each with your Approbation would be blest;
For the charm'd Nymphs desire as much to please,
As did the three contending Goddesses,
That bless'd young *Paris* in the mirtle Grove,
With the nice Choice of Grandure Wit and Love.
They would appear all eager of Success, ⎫
But are more cautious, cause their Charms less, ⎬
Besides they are resolv'd they'll not undress: ⎭
They've only yet their mystick Charms display'd,
And entertain'd you in a Masquerade;
But beg you would not take the Niceness ill,
For they resolve to wear their Vizards still;
May the soft Riddle never be explain'd,
Left the neglected blush to be disdain'd;
Should they divide; their Charms would be too small,
Were they Celestial; You would merit all.
Yes, lovely Youth, those mightier Charms of thine,
Deserve not only what, but all that is divine:
E're Nature form'd you, she in you design'd

Per-

Perfection far beyond all human Kind:
But scorn'd Materials from her common **Store**,
Travers'd her pregnant Universe all 'ore;
Pick'd up each softer *Atome* as she went;
Took too those bright ones next the Firmament.
Thus richly furnish'd she the Work began,
And joy'd to find it would be more than Man;
With utmost Care did every Charm encrease,
And e're she would compleat the Beauteous Piece,
Dip'd her nice Pencil in the liquid Light,
Varnish'd the whole, till Gods themselves less bright,
Each Deity deceiv'd with what was done,
Bestow'd some Gift and thought you was his own:
So liberally they gave; in you we see,
All their Perfections in Epitome.
No Wonder our weak Sex is charm'd to love
That Form which might the pleasing Object prove
Of all the wishing Female Court above:
'Tis they alone must for your Heart contend,
Your triple Nymph no farther doth pretend,
Than to adore the Glories they commend;
They are resolv'd they will remain intire,
Not run the Hazard of dilated Fire;
To other Swains their single Power might move,
And they neglecting charm to more than Love.

They

To Marina.

They know your Worth; so the deserving three
Will joyn, and be one *Delia* to thee;
Let one *Idea* fill thy grateful Breast,
Think they are so, in that Mistake they're blest.

To Marina.

PLague to thy Husband, scandal to thy Sex,
   Whose wearying Tongue does every Ear
                                          (perplex;
False to thy own false Soul, thou dost declare,
How Lust and Pride do Reign and Revel there,
Tell the World too, how nicely Chast you are.
This dull compulsive Virtues own'd; for who,
With one so odious would have ought to do?
But this Misfortune you too oft condole,
Whilst loosest Thoughts debauch your willing Soul
Thy best Discourse is but meer Ribaldry,
Telling how fond all that e're see you, be:
And loving all thy self, think'st all in Love with
With pious Heart thou studiest Vanity,   (thee.
And talk'st obscene by rules of Modesty.

Thus Sins nick-nam'd speak the infernal Saint,
Whose shining Robes are tawdry Cloaths and Paint,
Extravagance and Cheats you mark for Wit,
Thou abstract of Contention, Fraud and Spite.
If *Socrates* could have made choise of thee,
Thou would'st have baffled his Philosophy,
And turn'd his Patience to a Lunacy.
The restless Waters of the raging Sea,
Are a serene and halcion Stream to thee:
They keep their Banks and sometimes can be still,
Thou art all Tempest, know'st no bounds in Ill.
Pride, Lust, Contention, reign and yet repine,
Vesuvius Noise and Flame has less of Hell than thine.

Euterpe: *The Lyrick Muse*, On the Death of John Dryden, *Esq*;

An ODE.

I.

Soft *Euterpe*, sweetest of the *Nine*,
  The most Inspiring, and the most Divine,
 By my own Lyre rais'd to extatick Joy

Full

Euterpe: *The Lyrick Muse*, &c.

Full of kind Influence expecting fate,
When tuneful *Dryden* would my Aid implore,
Who with gay Transports did my Gifts employ,
And meanest Thoughts above my Notes did soar.
But strait a dismal, and unwelcome Sound,
Fill'd all th' Æthereal Courts around,
Great Dryden *is no more*.
But like the common things in mortal State,
Lost in th' impartial Gulf of an inevitable Fate,
At the dread News Grief all my Lustre veil'd,
I broke my harmonious *Harp* and *Lute*,
Threw by my softning ever-charming Flute,
Not the least glympse of Joy appears,
No radiant Nymphs about my Pallace wait,
Nor drink I any *Nectar* but my Tears.

II.

I with profoundest Cause, and Sorrow mourn,
Over my *Dryden*'s sacred Urn:
He was my greatest Glory, only boast,
Through him I let ungrateful Mankind know,
What mighty Wonders I could do,
But now, like him, to the inferior World I'm lost.

Euterpe: *The Lyrick Muse*, &c.

I taught Him all the softer Airs of Love,
And Anthems so divine; he'll find the same above.
With an auspicious Pride I did dispense
My mighty Favours, when *He* did implore,
  From my pregnant unexhausted Store,
  Of tuneful Fancies, and harmonious Sense.
When I with gentle Fire have warm'd the Breast,
The Soul with pleasing Raptures bles't,
The sacred Flame in ev'ry part does shine.
  The *Product*, like the *Source*, is all divine,
Poetry's not th' effect of Art, or Wine, or Love,
Tho' *They* sometimes the Gift improve,
  Nor is the warmth that Poets Breasts inspire,
Vinum Dæmonum, but Celestial Fire.
A God-like Ray enlightning from above;
As decent Measures, regular Motions be
  Through all the tuneful Universe,
  And speak in all a glorious Harmony,
  Ev'n so the mystick Numbers of melodious Verse,
Are of th' intellectual World the sacred Symmetry.

Dryden

III.

Dryden I chose of all the tuneful Throng,
His Soul with Ardour fill'd fit for immortal Song;
Learn'd him all Lyrick Arts of Poetry,
Such as might with Celestial Notes agree;
Which his Industry did improve,
In Celebrations, Elegies and Love,
And ev'ry Theme which his commanding Pen
(would try
With strength of Judgment, and profoundest Sense,
With sparkling Wit, gay Fancy, Eloquence,
His Verse did all abound:
In him alone was found
The much desir'd, aim'd at Excellence.
In ev'ry Line magnificent or sweet,
Like *OVID soft*, or else like *VIRGIL great*.
Orpheus magnetick Harp less Pow'r cou'd boast,
All *Rage*, unless in *Love* when e'er he sung was *lost*.
Above 'em all he rais'd his matchless Lays,
Glory of *Britain*, and Wits Empire too,
Which tho' the Subjects are but Few,

Did justly wreath him with deserved Bays:
　　The verdant Diadem which Laureats Crown,
　　Ne'er look'd so fresh as when he put it on,
Then like his Lines with Godlike-lustre shone.

IV.

With a Superior and victorious Grace
　　　The sacred Place,
He did almost unenvy'd assume,
　I, pleas'd to see the Branches spread
　　　O're his triumphant Head,
　　　From th' *Helicon* Spring
　　　　Did Water bring,
Sprinkled them oft that they might ever bloom.
　　But, oh! they cou'd not stand the Rage,
　Of an ill-natur'd and Lethargick Age,
　Who spight of *Wit* wou'd *stupidly* be Wise,
　　All noble Raptures, Extasies despise,
And only Plodders after Sense will Prize.
　　They from his meritorious Brow
　　　Th' exalted Laurel tear,
　　Which none but he could justly wear,
And He must suffer *Abdication* too.

　　　　　　　　　　　　　　With

V.

With Him they did suppress all lofty flights of Poe-
All melting Airs, and rapt'ring Harmony, (try.
But this Revenge, let Mankind take from me.
   If any dare on *Dryden*'s Death to Write,
   Not to express their Grief, but shew their Wit,
   I the ambitious Purpose will Reverse,
     Deny my Aid,
   And so shall each inspiring Maid.
   Resolving ungrateful Man that could con-
     Such noble Excellence in Him.   (temn
     Shall never more the Blessing know,
We'll ne'r again our Influence bestow.
Tho' 'tis pretended to adorn his Herse.
(Unless the generous *Montague* implore,
Then in him shall all our Glories shine as
                (heretofore.)
   But to express our own immortal Love,
   We'll Solemnize Great *Dryden*'s Obsequies
                (above,
   Our Grief such Emphasis shall bear,
   As no Corporeal Organs can declare,
And one Eternal Sigh spread thro' the Extended
                (Air.

Terpsichore: *A Lyrick Muse, On the Death of* John Dryden, *Esq; extempore.*

JUST as the Gods were listening to my Strains,
   And thousand Loves danc'd o're the Æthereal
                                       Plains;
With my own radiant Hair my Harp I strung,
And in glad Consort all my Sisters Sung;
An universal Harmony above,
Inspir'd us all with Gaiety and Love.
A horrid Sound dash'd our immortal Mirth,
Wafted by Sighs, from the unlucky Earth.
(Who'd think celestial Forms should Sorrows know,
Or sympathize with sad Events below?
But by our great immortal Selves we do.
For when the loud unwelcome Message spread,
With dismal Accents tuneful, *Dryden*'s dead,
All our gay Joys in haste affrighted fled.
A sullen Gloom seiz'd all the Gods around,
My feeble Hand no more the Lyre could sound:
And all the soft young Loves with drooping Wings,
Lisp't their Concern, and my neglected Strings;

Terpsichore: *A Lyrick Muse.*

Trembl'd themselves into a mournful Air,
Then Sight and Husht into a sad Despair.
There let them ever unreguarded lye,
Apollo's too, do's cease its Harmony.
He with us sacred Nymphs profusely Mourns,
With us the least desire of Respite scorns;
Intire eternal Grief our Beings seize
For him who best could us and Mankind please.
Great *Dryden*, in whose vast capacious Mind,
Our utmost Pow'r did fit Reception find;
Which Favours he did generously dispense,
Joy'd the glad World with his amazing Sense,
And like us too diffus'd his Influence;
His Genius would such Inspiration bear,
That his Illustrious Lines did not appear
As if our Product, but our Selves were there.
Mourn ye forsaken Worlds, you'l ne're again
Be blest with so Divine, so great a Swain.
In you no more let tuneful Mirth be found,
The very Spheres shall cease their wonted Sound,
And every Orb stop its harmonious round:
All Nature hush as if intranc't she lay,
Sunk in old Chaos e'er the inlight'ning Ray
Of Heaven awak'd her in the first-born Day.

With

With such still Horrour let's our sorrows bear,
Lest Sighs in time, harmonious should appear.
If e'er to write again is Man's intent,
(Uncall'd on let us silently lament,)
And take his Works, for an Eternal President,

The Platonick.

PReposterous Fate, let me accuse thee now,
(What means this Mirtle on the Cypress bough;)
Ah! why thus treacherously in Friendship drest,
Hast thou to Love, betray'd my unweary Breast?
Amintor's latest Breath did recommend,
Me to the care of his once dearest Friend;
We the kind fatal Orders did persue,
And for his sake I strove to Love him too:
Methoughts *Amintor* did his Thanks Proclaim,
Look'd down and smil'd, and authoriz'd my Flame.
Bid me my greatest Favours there bestow,
Where he lov'd best (excepting me) below;
But my ill Fate, th' obedient purpose crost,
Duty was soon in Inclination lost;

For

The Platonick.

For oh! I find the generous Probation,
Has now commenc'd an unsuspected Passion.
I would my Friendship to the height improve,
Which unawars did sublimate to Love;
So some well meaning Votaries in Religion,
Run their Devotion up to Superstition:
But from the utmost Error I'll be free,
And not degenerate to Idollatry.
Confess the kind Platonick at the most,
And make my Passion not my Blush, but Boast;
I do not wish him in these careless Arms,
Let me but gaze at distance on his Charms;
To view that softning Air, that Voice to hear,
Is all the Bliss my temperate Soul wou'd share.
But then be ever present ever kind,
Joy to my Eyes and Pleasure to my Mind.
I shall be blest if you'll allow but this,
Shou'd you be kinder, t'would abate my Bliss:
My elevated Flame needs no supply,
But the nice subtil Fewel of the Eye:
In Contemplation all my Pleasure lies,
My Joys are pure Ideal Extacies:
The Lip or Hand are not enough refin'd,
With Looks and Smiles let me regale my Mind
'Tis all my softest Wishes e'er design'd.

Love

Love like the sacred Tree which *Eden* grac't,
To entertain the sight is only plac't;
Safely we gaze, but if we venter on,
To touch and tast, we blush and are undone.

The Emulation.

SAY Tyrant Custom, why must we obey,
The impositions of thy haughty Sway;
From the first dawn of Life, unto the Grave,
Poor Womankind's in every State, a Slave.
The Nurse, the Mistress, Parent and the Swain,
For Love she must, there's none escape that Pain;
Then comes the last, the fatal Slavery,
The Husband with insulting Tyranny
Can have ill Manners justify'd by Law;
For Men all join to keep the Wife in awe.
Moses who first our Freedom did rebuke,
Was Marry'd when he writ the Pentateuch;
They're Wise to keep us Slaves, for well they know,
If we were loose, we soon should make them, so.
We yeild like vanquish'd Kings whom Fetters bind,
When chance of War is to Usurpers kind;

Sub-

Submit in Form; but they'd our Thoughts controul,
And lay restraints on the impassive Soul:
They fear we should excel their sluggish Parts,
Should we attempt the Sciences and Arts.
Pretend they were design'd for them alone,
So keep us Fools to raise their own Renown;
Thus Priests of old their Grandeur to maintain,
Cry'd vulgar Eyes would sacred Laws Prophane.
So kept the Mysteries behind a Screen,
There Homage and the Name were lost had they
(been seen:
But in this blessed Age, such Freedom's given,
That every Man explains the Will of Heaven;
And shall we Women now sit tamely by,
Make no excursions in Philosophy,
Or grace our Thoughts in tuneful Poetry?
We will our Rights in Learning's World maintain,
Wits Empire, now, shall know a Female Reign;
Come all ye Fair, the great Attempt improve,
Divinely imitate the Realms above:
There's ten celestial Females govern Wit,
And but two Gods that dare pretend to it;
And shall these finite Males reverse their Rules,
No, we'll be Wits, and then Men must be Fools.

To Mr. Yalden, *on his Temple of Fame*, Extempore.

HAD *Gloʻester* liv'd, and made his Actions,
With the united Glories of his Line, shine,
He'd less Immortal been than in these lays of thine.
Not only Royal Tears adorn his Urn,
But you have taught the Subjects all to mourn:
Your melting Lines, make conscious Passion vent
More solemn Griefs, than common Nature meant
Soft are thy strains as his once moving Tongue,
Fond *Venus* lose was less divinely Sung;
Amintor, *Colin*, young *Alexis* too,
Justly resign the Prize, to mightier you.
The weeping Nymphs, all throw their Cypress down,
With eager Hands wreath your victorious Crown;
You from whom Kings such Glories do receive,
Yet to your self superior Honours give,
Since they but lye, where you'll for ever live.

On the Death of William III, King of England.

YE mighty Nine, suspend your sacred Fire,
　　Strong Grief like Love can coldest Breasts in-
Nor shall I want *Castilian* Waters here,　　(spire;
For every line can Boast an ardent Tear.
But if the artless Sorrows of my Breast,
In numbers fail, my Sighs shall speak the rest;
With untun'd Lyre, and slacken'd Nerves I Sing,
Yet with a Pious hast, my humble Tribute bring
Of Grief immense, an equal Theme of Praise,
But oh! what Pen can worthy Trophies raise.
Great *William* now our Annals proudest Boast,
Whose dawning Glories joy'd the *Belgick* Coast;
When at *Seneff*, he stem'd the impetuous Strife,
And Laurels flourish'd in th' Bloom of Life.
Nor did his Triumphs end where they begin,
Heaven gave fresh Scenes to act his Glories in;
Ammon's nor *Cæsar*'s Fame, must here contend,
The Valour had an avaricious End,
Thy fought to win the World, he to defend.
Britannia's Wrongs his willing Aid demand,
He hazards all, to save the sinking Land;

Not

Not Winter Seas the generous Prince restrain,
Nor num'rous Hosts on *Albion*'s shining Plain:
No threat'ning Danger terrour can afford,
When Justice calls for his avenging Sword.
Boldly he march'd to dare th' oppressing Foe,
Nor Conquest fear'd, when Heaven directs the (Blow;

Frighted Commanders, quit their guilty Post,
'Tis *Orange* comes, they know the Field is lost.
None dare approach the mighty Victor's Face,
But such as safely sue for his Imbrace;
With blooming Palms the regal Seat obtain'd,
He saves those Rights his Valour had regain'd.
But soon *Hibernia*'s insulting Foes,
Calls forth the Hero from his short repose;
(Not thirst of Empire, Mankind to inslave,
Nor fights so much to Conquer, as to save:)
Led by a tenderness his Courage moves,
Like *Mars*'s Chariot, drawn by *Venus* Doves.
With Pride great *Neptune* bears the Royal freight,
Where the defenceless Isles, Impatient wait,
And look from him, as Heaven their Nations fate.
Th' undaunted Warrior like the God of Arms,
Shines thro' the Field and every Souldier warms.

In vain the *Boyne* would Victory delay,
Nor can its Streams their generous Heat allay;
Boldly they Plunge the bright propitious Flood,
And in the Waves like arm'd *Tryton* stood.
The amphibious Squadrons charge upon their Foes,
Nor in the Liquid Plain their ardor loose:
But with united force the Fight persue,
Till laurels load the daring Monarch's brow.
Soon as the Land was safe his Weapons cease,
With his victorious Hand, he seal'd their Peace;
Mourn all ye injur'd Realms your helpless Cause,
No Sword can Succour you like kind *Nassaus*,
And that's for ever sheath'd —— no more can save,
That mighty Arm, lies useless in the Grave.

   Come widdow'd *Belgia* with sad *Britain* join,
Unite your Tears and swell the gentle *Boyne*;
She'll rise in Silver heaps at *Nassaus* Name,
With Pride her Streams are conspicious of his Fame,
And all her wondering Banks with Joy resound
                             (the same.
But when your flowing Eyes declare his Death,
She will no more her sporting Waters heave;

But sadly sink into her mournful Cell,
In subteranean Murmurs hast to tell,
At *Neptune*'s Court how his great Master fell,
Each *Neried* strait her Sea green Tresses tares,
And swells the Ocean with their flowing Tears:
The *Trytons*

Unfinisht.

To N. Tate, *Esq; on his Poem on the Queen's Picture, Drawn by* Closterman.

Hail mighty Poet, mighty Painter too,
 Since to thy strokes his equal Lines we owe;
The sister Arts, are now a Mistery
And Painture here, has brought forth Poetry.
Th' inspiring Shade, seems life itself refin'd,
And all Heavens goodness coppy'd in her Mind;
So justly each performs his nicer Part,
As speaks their Skill, yet Beauties without Art:
The emmulative Ink, bright as the Paint,
This shows the Queen and that describes the Saint.

We

To Mr. Tate, &c.

We prize in others still the lasting Soul,
But ye have Here, immortaliz'd the whole:
Speak great *Apollo* thou alone canst tell,
Whether the Pencil or the Pen excell.

Brib'd by the native Ardour of my Breast,
My Muse no longer will their worth contest:
But must to *Tate* yeild the superior Crown,
Who has compleated *Closterman*'s Renown,
And in his Praise reverberates his own.
But oh! what Trophies of immortal Fame,
Are justly rais'd to sacred *Anna*'s Name.
Britannia knew not she was half so blest,
Till the Diviner Raptures of my Breast,
Declar'd what else could ne'er have been exprest.
Her Glory shines in thy Pathetick Lays,
So *Colin* once Sung fam'd *Elizia* Praise;
Long may thy *Astræa Albion*'s Scepter bear,
Whilst she the Crown may you the Laurel wear.

To my much valu'd Friend Moneses.

Great *Pæan* now thy strongest Rays dispense,
Give *Virgils* Flights and *Dryden*'s Eloquence:
All the fam'd Bards of sacred Poetry,
Let their bright Flames revive again in me.
Inspire my Breast whilst I his Praise rehearse,
Whose worth deserves thy own immortal Verse;
I sing *Moneses* whom the Gods ordain'd,
To show their Form, e'er 'twas by Sin prophan'd:
He is all Goodness, Mercy, Justice, Truth,
Has all the Charms without the vice of Youth.
These are the Native Beauties of his Soul,
While every Art and Grace adorns the whole:
Obliging is his Mein, his Judgment strong,
A flowing Wit directs his pleasing Tongue;
And each inchanting Accent which we hear,
Like airs Divine Transport the list'ning Ear.
Not *Orpheus* Harp, not yet *Amphion*'s Lyre,
Could with more Sweetness or more force inspire:
Oh! what Infernal Magick Mortals bind,
That his instructive Voice can't move the Mind,
And calm the raging Follies of Mankind.

(The passive Stones obey'd less powerful Sound,
For in their heaps was no resisting Atoms found;)
Not greater Pride or Joys did *Ammon* move,
When by the Shrine, pronounc'd the Son of *Jove*:
Then are the Transports my blest Soul attend,
That I can call the brave *Moneses* Friend.
Moneses whom *Apollo* has design'd,
With his own Arts, to Heal and Charm Mankind;
Fain would I still persue my wondrous Song,
But oh! fast the bright Ideas throng,
Stifl'd in Raptures e'er they reach my Tongue:
So when with greatest Zeal we Heaven accost,
Our Notions in all Extacies are lost,
We utter least, where it deserves the most.

FINIS.

The fond Shepherdess.
A PASTORAL.

Daphne, and *Larinda.*

BY a soft murmuring Stream in heat of Day,
Remote from all, the sad *Larinda* lay
Beneath the spreading Willows gloomy Shade,
(A cool recess by careful Nature made;)
There lost in thought, soothing her amorous Pains,
Forgot her Flocks, and business of the Plains.
The Shepherds wonder'd that she stay'd so long,
Each left his Pipe, and stopt his rural Song
Searching th' adjacent Woods and Groves around,
Impatient all, till they *Larinda* found.
The careful *Daphne* distant Vallies try'd
And there with Joy the pensive Wand'rer spy'd:
Ran to her Arms with a transported Hast
A thousand times, the sighing Nymph imbrac'd.

The fond Shepherdess.

Daph. Tell me, said she, what makes you all (neglect,
Nor now from Sun, or Wolves your Sheep protect,
But let them wander o're th' unbounded Plain,
Scorch'd by the one, and by the other Slain?
Tho' you may now the greatest numbers Boast
Unheeded thus your Flocks will soon be lost.
Nay of your self too, you are careless grown
Shun all the Nymphs to Muse in Shades alone:
Your head's not now, with Rosy Chaplets drest,
No fragrant Poesy decks your pensive Breast,
Nor decent Rushes strow'd beneath the Shade,
Where smiling once with sporting Lambs you (play'd.
The little Bird you fondly taught to Sing,
Releas'd from Cage, and trusted to its Wing:
You tore each tender Sonnet you have made,
Wish'd the Pipe broke, when sighing *Strephon* play'd.
Ah! why thus peevish? Can your faithful Heart
Conceal a Grief from her, who'd bear a Part?

Lar. No kind Inquirer when with cares opprest,
I still repose in yours, my weary'd Breast;

But

But I have now, no Secret to reveal,
I've lost some Lambs, as all the Plains can tell.
At the approach of last refreshing Show'r,
In haste I ran to yonder well fenc'd Bow'r;
In the kind shelter too long Sleeping lay,
Or Thief, or Wolf, my Darling stole away.

Daph. Do not evade the Truth, but be sincere;
For long ere this, your Eyes did sorrows wear,
Besides, I saw you ere you was awake
Disturb'd you slept, with eager accents spake,
(Oh! my *Exalis* will you leave me.) Then
Foulded your tender Arms, and Slept agen.
Nay, do not blush at the discover'd Truth,
Too well I know you Love that charming Youth,
Oft you together, your mixt Flocks did feed,
Delight your selves with his harmonious Reed.
If any Straglers, from your Folds did run;
Each, would the others seek, neglect their own;
Such mutual kindnesses the Soul indear,
Exalis was your Joy, and you was all his Care.

Lar. Oh! Name him not; yes, ever sound that
(Name,
For 'tis in vain to hide th' undoing Flame.

The fond Shepherdess.

I Love, nay rather the bright Youth adore,
Eccho ne'r doated on *Narcissus* more;
Nor had he half of my *Exalis* Charms
To tempt the Nymph to his resisting Arms
'Mongst all the Swains. Speak *Daphne*, have you seen
A Shape so fine, or such a pleasing Mein,
Fair as the Doves which o're our Cottage flys,
Soft as their Down, and just such lovely Eyes.
His flowing Locks in amorous Ringlets twine,
Like the Young curling Tendrils of the Vine:
Not *Philomel*'s soft Voice, like his, can move,
His ev'ry accent has an Air of Love;
All the gay Chaunters of the welcome Spring,
Like me, are hush'd and joy'd; if he but speak or
(Sing
A Breath as Sweet, as when the Evening Breeze
Salutes us from yon Grove of spicy Trees;
His lovely Smiles, soft Brightness do display,
Like glowing Blushes of the infant Day.
When o'er the Mountain-tops the blooming Light,
Darts its Young Beams to th' early Gazers sight,
Like *Pan* himself, the Glory of the Woods,
While other Swains seem Mean, attendant Gods:
Then who such mighty Charms can e'er resist?
Charms like my Love, too great to be exprest.

Daph.

The fond Shepherdess

Daph. Oh fatal Power of Love, that thus can
⟨seize
The nice *Larinda*, whom no Swain could please;
But now a Slave, worse than e'er sigh'd for you,
You doat to Passion; nay, Distraction too.
Tell me, sad soften'd Nymph, how long your Breast,
Has been by these too mighty Griefs opprest?

Lar. Yes, I will tell you; my unweary'd Tongue,
Speaking of him, can ne'er think Ages long.
Daphne, you know what time the lovely Swain,
With his Blest Flocks, has grac'd our happy Plain:
From the first Hour, he did obliging prove;
(I little thought, to pay him back in Love)
He within bounds, my wandring Lambs would
⟨keep,
When I was weary, gladly Fold my Sheep.
And as I rested, in the verdant Shade,
On oaten Reeds melodious Airs he play'd.
The listning Shepherds not far distant stand,
Pleas'd, and yet envying that dear skilful Hand:
Not *Pan*'s immortal Pipe, could more Inspire,
Or glad the Plains, than my *Exalis* Lyre.

It Joy'd all Hearts, to mine did Fatal prove,
And taught my liftning Soul, the way to Love.
On a fresh Bank, by a clear Fountain side,
(Where *Flora* smil'd with gaudy vernal Pride.
Phœbus was gone, to *Thetis* yielding Arms,
But *Luna* left her Dear, *Endymion*'s Charms;
Smil'd o'er the Grove, scarce Day it self more
(Bright,
And thro' the Boughs, sprinkled the Shade with
Light.)
There with gay Innocence, supine we sate,
Hear'd injur'd *Philomel* her Wrongs relate,
But no forwarning Bird told my approaching
(Fate.
Then as I lean'd on the enamel'd Ground,
I cropt the fragrant Flowers all around;
The various Colours, artfully I plac'd,
And with them pleas'd *Exalis* Bosom dress'd.
To him a Crook and Beachen bowl I gave,
(Did with my careful Hand the last Ingrave,)
One side, with various Silvan Nymphs, I grac'd,
And on the other *Pan* and *Flora* plac'd.
Take these, said I; for all the generous Care,
In which, so oft, my Flocks and I did share;

And

The fond Shepherdess.

And when I die, *Exalis* take them too,
Tho' loft to me, they'll Joy to be with you;
Like me, they'r wonted to your gentle Call;
I only grieve their number is fo fmall.
He fmil'd to hear the tender things I faid,
While grateful looks his pleafing Anfwers made;
And then half Blufhing on his Mufick play'd,
Lift'ning; that dear undoing Face I view'd,
To catch each Smile, which kindly was beftow'd.
But Oh! too long, too long I gazeing fate;
My Soul, with foftning Airs, prepar'd by Fate,
Took the Impreffion of that charming Face,
Which, Smiling, darted Glory round the Place:
A thoufand Loves in amorous Fires dreft,
With one dear look pierc'd my too ready Breaft:
I thought Heaven's Brightnefs in thofe radiant Eyes,
And blufht, and fainted at the foft furprize;
Yet hop'd the mighty Tranfport would be o'er,
And the gay Youth but pleafe as heretofore:
But oh! you may as foon yon Mountain move,
As raze out the immortal Characters of Love.

Daph. Then with what caution fhould we guard
(the Breaft,
And the firft glimmering of the Flame refift?

A Flame, so fatal, that it doth Destroy,
In sad *Larinda*, every thought of Joy:
If all kind Breasts are with such torture mov'd,
May I ne'er Love, nor ever be be lov'd?
No; rather let me and my Flocks, be drove
From this fresh Pasture, and delightful Grove;
Confin'd to barren Sands and scorchhing Sun,
Where no Shades near, nor useful Waters run;
Fainted with wandring o'er the fiery Dust,
Famish'd for Food, Parch'd up with Heat and
                                         (Thirst:
My darling Lambs around me bleat Complaints;
I void of all, that can relieve their Wants:
Yet I'd endure this piercing Scene of Woe;
These utmost ills poor *Daphne*'s State can know:
Rather then Love, should my gay Breast subdue,
With such soft amorous Griefs as torture you;
Ah why, would you indulge the fond desire,
And not at first Stifle the growing Fire?

  Lar. At its Approach, with tender warmth were Blest,
The lambent Flame plays, with the sporting Breast,
And give such Joys, none would, or can resist.

The fond Shepherdess.

No Lover yet, could e'er of Forecast Boast,
Percieve no Ruin, till they know they'r lost:
Now with the fondest Flames of Love I burn,
Doom'd to the certain Curse of no return.
When to the fickle Youth, I own'd I lov'd,
His Flocks he straight to *Ida*'s Plains remov'd;
He ne'er returns, to see how mine do fare,
Nor I, nor they, are now no more his Care.
Curse on my Love, which did itself disclose,
By what should keep, I did my Charmer lose;
Now I no more must see his lovely Face,
Hear his inchanting Voice, his melting Lays;
Lays, which in coldest Breasts would Raptures (move
Make the Soul Gay, and ev'ry Pulse beat Love.
Gods! how he'd look and Smile; how was I blest,
When the charm'd Youth, lean'd on my willing (Breast,
Spake things as soft, as the kind Hand he prest?
But now all's lost, I rage beyond redress,
(He'l ne'er return, nor I e'er Love him less.)
First, I was cautious to conceal my Flame,
Now every Breath repeats his dear Lov'd Name:
I carve, *Exalis* on each smooth bark'd Tree,
That if the mangl'd Woods could vocal be,
They'd surely Curse my fond Barbarity.

Each

The fond Shepherdess.

Each sigh has such a tender Emphasis,
As moves Compassion, in all Breasts but his:
For all the Swains are Conscious that I Love;
Each Tow'ring Hill, and every humble Grove;
I've tir'd them all, with my incessant Crys,
Ecchoes grown faint, repeating of my sighs:
My Sighs, whose force move ev'ry Bough to
(Mourn,
In pitying murmurs that I've no return:
Oft do I run to the inviting Shade,
Where first his pleasing Smiles, my Soul betray'd;
There lay me down in the dear sacred Place,
Which kindly once, his lovely Form did Grace;
Then weep his Absence; Rage and Rave in vain,
For oh! I ne'er must be so Blest again;
I try if Slumbers will afford Relief,
But as they sooth, so they augment my Grief.
I clasp him then in my glad wishing Arms,
Gaze on his Eyes, and feast me with his Charms;
But when awake; I rage to find him gone,
To lose the lovely Prize, I thought I'd won.
Search ev'ry Corner of the winding Grove;
Ask every Shade, to give me back my Love.
There silent all, and empty of such Bliss;
In vain I seek for Joys, I'm doom'd to miss:
Too

The fond Shepherdess.

So well *Exalss* knows he gives delight,
But he Industriously avoids my sight,
Tho' Prayers, and Tears, and Gifts, and bloom-
            (ing Love invite.

He absents, to cure me 'tis in vain,
For still his bright Idea doth remain,
And ev'ry moment Charms me into Pain.

Other Youths may moderate Passion move;
As he's all lovely, I'm all over Love:
Soft to all else, insensible I seem,
And only know I'm something doats on him
If I would count my Sheep into the Fould,
Forget their number ere they half are told;
And when the Nymphs my heedlesness do blame,
I answer all, by sighing of his Name.
Farewel, my *Daphne*, I must leave thee now,
One pitying Tear, on my sad Fate bestow;
Return thou Glory of the Joyful Grove,
May'st thou be Blest, for may'st thou never Love.
Farewel my once lov'd Flocks, my rural Store;
Larinda now will ne'er regard you more.
But wing'd with Love, to *Ida*'s Plains I'll fly:
Find my *Exalis* out; to see me die.

No longer on my tedious Griefs I'll wait,
That melting Name so often I'll repeat,
Till the soft sound dissolve the Knot of Fate.
Curss'd by his Absence, Life is tedious grown;
Now he shall see what his neglect has done.
While I can gaze, it shall be on his Charms,
And tho' not live; die in those lovely Arms;
But if he envying,. think that Bliss too great,
I'll sigh my Soul out, at his careless Feet;
Then let one pitying Look but Grace my Death,
I'll Bless the Cause, with my expiring Breath.

Hear me Great *Pan*, *Sylvanus*, all ye Gods,
Whose sacred Power, protects the Plains and
(Woods,
Hear my last Prayer; (to you I oft did Bow,
With Milk and Hony, made your Altars Flow.)
While my sad Shade, mourns in the dusky Grove,
Releas'd from Life; (but not the Pains of Love.)
Bless my *Exalis*, let him know no Cares,
Increase his plenteous Herds, and peaceful Years;
From Fox and Wolf, preserve his tender Lambs,
And with Twin-births, enrich the fruitful Dams.
When his fair Flocks the Shearers care demands,
Luxuriant Fleeces, tire their num'rous Hands.
The

The fond Shepherdess.

The industrious Bees load their melifluous Hive,
And all his rural Wealth, beyond his Wishes
(thrive.
But above all, ye Gods, regard him most,
Save him from parching Sun and piercing Frost:
Shelter him safe, e'er any Storm appear,
And let him be to you, as to *Larinda* dear.

I bounteous Gods, for plenty first bespoke,
Now for his Pleasures, *Flora* thee invoke:
Let my soft Prayers, thy vernal Glories bring,
Bless *Ida*'s Plains, with glad eternal Spring:
The Pasture gay, no hurtful Weeds be found,
But Pancies, Hyacinths, 'ore spread the Ground;
Mirtle and Firr make every Decent mound:
Let lofty Cedars and the stately Pine,
With mingling Boughs in mutual Shades combine:
Then the delicious Eglantine and Rose,
With fragrant Jess'mine humbler Bowers compose
(Where the dear Youth may oft supinely Rest,
With pleasing Dreams, in Golden slumbers Blest,)
When Heat or Thirst, to flowing Streams invite,
Let sporting Naiads entertain his Sight;
Birds chearful Notes, the Woods and Vallies fill,
From spicy Trees which odourous Gums distil.

The fond Shepherdess.

Amongst these Aromaticks rich Fruits plac'd,
Fair to the Sight, as those *Hesperian* grac'd,
Which both Invite, and Please the longing Tast.
The cluster'd Boughs, Complaisantly recline,
As if they Joy'd the Gatherers hand to Join,
And all the choicest, still my Love be thine.

And when in Honour, Goddess, to thy Name,
The joyful Swains, in sports their Thanks Proclaim,
Whether they Pipe, or Dance, or Sing, or Play,
May my *Exalis*, bear the Prize away.
From Shepherd's Hands the welcome Garland
(wear,
For oh! I Grudge the Nymphs shou'd come so
(near)
Yet if 'twill please him best; then smiling come,
And with glad Voices sing the Victor home;
With choicest Flowers strow all the joyful Path,
Gay as his Looks, sweet as his tuneful Breath.
Then some kind Nymph the fragrant Pave-
(ment take
His pressing Feet, give double Odours back;
Each Rose, *Anemone*, more Beauteus make:
Let them fresh Mixture with the *Cypress* have,
Then strow them all on my untimely Grave.

They

The fond Shepherdess.

They too were Lovers once, tho' now transform'd,
May I like them, to some kind Plant be turn'd;
And when *Exalis*, next in Triumph's led,
Make Poseys for his Breast, and Garlands for his
(Head:
Let not the Nymph upbraid, when shes return'd,
My Grave is fill'd, and grac'd with what he scorn'd:
Left, he relenting, should one Moment grieve,
To save a Sigh, I'd be condemn'd to Live:
With raging Madness, mourn my absent Bliss,
And with my Cries wound every Ear but his.

Here the Nymph fainted with excess of Grief,
And careful *Daphne*, strove to give Relief.

FINIS.

For Product Safety Concerns and Information please contact our EU representative GPSR@taylorandfrancis.com
Taylor & Francis Verlag GmbH, Kaufingerstraße 24, 80331 München, Germany